THE
PROBLEM
RE-SOLVING
SOLUTION

Transform Life's Problems Into Clarity, Balance, & Momentum

MICHAEL ALCANTARA

Published by Alcantara Creative Holdings (ACH)
ISBN Paperback: 979-8-9940260-0-7
ISBN HardBack: 979-8-9940260-1-4
ISBN EBook: 979-8-9940260-2-1
Library of Congress Control Number: 2026901745
Printed in the United States of America
First paperback edition, 2026

A portion of proceeds from this book supports charitable initiatives.

GBA BRIGHT FUTURES FOUNDATION

Vision Statement: Our vision is to create a future where every child has access to nutritious food, enabling them to thrive academically and reach their full potential without the burden of hunger.

Mission Statement: Our mission is to alleviate childhood hunger by providing access to healthy meals, promoting nutritional education, and fostering community partnerships to support the well-being and academic success of all children.

Purpose Statement: Driven by the belief that no child should go hungry, our purpose is to remove barriers to academic achievement by ensuring that every child has reliable access to nourishing meals. We are committed to addressing the root causes of food insecurity and building a community where every child can grow, learn, and thrive.

https://www.gbabrightfutures.org/

This book is dedicated to my caring mother my loving wife and life companion, Riza. Thank you, Mom, for raising me with the limited resources you had and making the necessary sacrifices to ensure a brighter future to come. Thank you, Riza, for believing in me, supporting me in my crazy plans and ideas.

To my children, who have been instrumental in my problems, challenges, and change, it is because of you that I am writing this book. I created this for you as a guide and manual as you navigate the world.

And to everyone who has contributed to my journey, my family, friends, coworkers, and those who are going through their own problem-re-solving journey, know you are not alone, and there is always a rainbow at the end.

"Nothing in this world can take the place of persistence. Talent will not; nothing is more common than unsuccessful men with talent. Genius will not; unrewarded genius is almost a proverb. Education will not; the world is full of education derelicts. Persistence and determination alone are omnipotent. The slogan "Press On! has solved and always will solve the problems of the human race."

Calvin Coolidge

ACKNOWLEDGEMENTS

I would like to acknowledge everyone who has helped me write this book, whether by brainstorming ideas or by sharing their life stories and examples. I appreciate everyone's feedback and responses. To Joseph Dunn, my first-level editor, I appreciate the support, brother! To Dr. Richard A. Singletary, my English as a Second Language Teacher, and my very first mentor. Who saw me before I could even speak for myself. To Alan Powers who kept me out of trouble and advised to keep my eyes on the prize. To everyone who took time to read my draft and offer feedback and support. To Larry Patterson, Asheley Pruett, Randy Diaz, Blake Eikenberry, Todd Mcallister, Joseph Feniza, Bogartha Soeprapto, Tabitha Pollardson, Geoffrey Stone. To my book coach, Neno Littlewood, from Writers Rebellion. To my copy line editor, Rachel Clair, from Book Bound Journey. To the Miblart team for design and formatting. To my Riverside Writers Group. Thank you for believing in me and pushing me towards my full potential. In the end, this is for all of us.

CONTENTS

INTRODUCTION 1

CHAPTER 1 MISSION: GOALS & OBJECTIVES 10

PRS IN PRACTICE: DEFINE YOUR MISSION 15

CHAPTER 2 MOTIVE: PURPOSE & IDENTITY 20

PRS IN PRACTICE: IDENTIFY YOUR MOTIVE. 25

CHAPTER 3 METHOD: SYSTEM & STRUCTURE. 28

PRS IN PRACTICE: ESTABLISHING PRS. 41

CHAPTER 4 MENTALITY: MINDSET & ATTITUDE 46

PRS IN PRACTICE: STRENGTHEN YOUR MENTALITY 84

CHAPTER 5 MODEL: BEHAVIOR & ACTIONS. 89

PRS IN PRACTICE: FIND YOUR QUADRANT 109

CHAPTER 6 MOVEMENT: FRAMEWORK & MOMENTUM. 114

PRS IN PRACTICE: BUILD YOUR MOMENTUM. 140

CHAPTER 7 MAPPING: APPROACHES & APPLICATIONS 145

PRS IN PRACTICE: MASTER YOUR DECISIONS 161

CHAPTER 8 MAINTENANCE: TOOLS & TECHNIQUES 166

PRS IN PRACTICE: SUSTAIN YOUR SYSTEM 202

CHAPTER 9 MASTERY: MY STORY OF TRANSFORMATION . . 208

PRS IN PRACTICE: WRITING THIS BOOK 214

CHAPTER 10: CONCLUSION & MOVING FORWARD 219

APPENDIX:THE PRS DAILY BLUEPRINT:

TURNING INSIGHT INTO ACTION 222

PROBLEM RE-SOLVING: DAILY WORKSHEET 226

INFLUENTIAL BOOKS FOR FURTHER STUDY 228

REFERENCES 230

ABOUT THE AUTHOR 232

INTRODUCTION

"To solve any problem, here are three questions to ask yourself: First, what could I do? Second, what could I read? And third, who could I ask?"
Jim Rohn

I always wanted to write a book. Just not this one. It was supposed to be fiction about an unknown hero in a faraway land, fighting off villains and saving his world from unseen evil. But life had other plans. It handed me real battles, complex problems, hard challenges, and major changes that no one could rescue me from. Somewhere along the way, I realized I wasn't equipped for the ride.

I started reading self-help and motivational books, trying to find answers. They gave me insight, discipline, and motivation, but something was still missing. I noticed a pattern in my life and in others around me. My friends, coworkers, and family were struggling. We were all wrestling with the same cycle of burnout, indecision, and overwhelm. We either took action too soon, waited too long, froze in fear, or burned out from doing too much. We were all busy but not balanced. There had to be a better way.

What I eventually realized was this: most of us aren't bad at solving problems—we're just solving the same version of them over and over again. We calm the symptoms, manage the stress, and move forward just enough to function. Then weeks, months, or years later, the same challenge shows up again in a different form. That's not failure. It's a sign that something deeper is asking for attention. This book doesn't dwell on that idea, but it does acknowledge it—because learning how to reengage problems with awareness is very different from reacting to them on autopilot.

This book was born from that realization and not from ambition but from necessity. I needed to understand life's chaos and build a way through it. I wanted to stop reacting and start resolving the challenges thrown my way. And I wasn't alone. Every person I met seemed to struggle with the same questions: Why does it feel like I'm doing everything right but still not moving forward? Am I doomed to keep repeating the same mistakes over and over again?

If you've ever felt stuck, overwhelmed, or unsure of your next step, this book is for you. It's for the overachievers who are exhausted, the dreamers who can't get started, the thinkers who hesitate, and the fighters who never stop pushing. It's for anyone searching for clarity, awareness, balance, and momentum. Even when that first step feels impossible.

My turning point came when I read *Who Moved My Cheese?* by Dr. Spencer Johnson. It was a simple story, but it hit me hard. I saw myself in the mouse named Scurry. He was always rushing to fix things, trying to outpace the problem, hoping speed alone could save me. But that constant motion often created more chaos. That sparked something in me. What if there was a better system? Something that informs me not just to act but to think, reflect, and move with purpose? I needed a solution and a system.

That question became *Problem Re-Solving Solution*. This book isn't about perfection or success but progress. Constant progress that doesn't stop. It's about learning to handle life's problems, challenges, and changes with awareness and balance. It's about recognizing your patterns first. Whether you overthink, avoid, rush, or over-commit. Then learning how to shift into a better rhythm.

This isn't just a book—it introduces the **Problem Re-Solving** System, or **PRS** for short. It's more than a theory; it's a blueprint for how to navigate the recurring ups and downs of life. The PRS system helps you get unstuck, create balance, build momentum, and handle problems with a clearer head and stronger heart. It weaves together mentality, frameworks, and practical tools so you can stop reacting and start re-solving problems effectively and efficiently. Before we go deeper, here's a simple way to use this book when you're facing any problem in your life.

- Identify what's bothering you. Name the problem clearly and honestly.
- Decide that you're ready to address it. A small commitment is enough to begin.
- Build awareness and clarity. Understand your thoughts, emotions, and starting point.
- Make a decision. Choose your direction — even if it's just your next move.
- Take one small intentional step. Progress begins with a single action.
- Stay balanced and keep momentum. Avoid overthinking or rushing; move steadily and mindfully.

- Re-solve problems. Adjust as life pushes back — growth is a loop, not a line.
- Reflect on lessons learned. Every challenge teaches you something for the next one.

Think of it this way. Solving a problem is like putting out a fire. It stops the immediate damage. Resolving the problem calms what's left behind. But re-solving asks a deeper question: why do fires keep starting in the first place? PRS is built for that level of thinking. It doesn't just help you fix what's burning—it helps you change how you respond, prepare, and move forward so the same problems don't keep reappearing in new forms. As you move through the chapters, you'll learn how to do each of these steps with more confidence, awareness, and control.

This book is designed to teach, educate, and mentor you on a step-by-step basis. It should feel natural to apply and has a top-down approach. It begins with a big picture, a mission, moves onto models and frameworks, and finally ends with approaches, tools, and techniques. The chapters are intentionally structured to do more than explain ideas. Each section follows a consistent pattern so you're never wondering what to do next or how to apply what you've learned. You'll move from understanding to action, from insight to implementation, with real examples drawn from my own life to show how these principles work outside of theory. It's meant to be practiced, reflected on, and revisited whenever life throws you off balance. Here is a list that sections are designed to include.

- A grounding quote. To set perspective and anchor the lesson emotionally.

- A visual or graphic if applicable. To help you see the concept, not just read about it.
- A core lesson. That explains the idea in plain language without jargon.
- Practical guidance. That shows how to apply the concept in real life.
- A personal example. Where I demonstrate how I've used these steps myself — imperfectly, but intentionally.

At the end of every chapter, we will start a **PRS in Practice** worksheet designed to reinforce quick reflection with short prompts to connect concepts emotionally and mentally, action exercise, or checklist with simple steps or questions to reinforce awareness and encourage action. You don't need to master everything in one pass. Read what you need, return when you're ready, and trust that clarity comes through thoughtful repetition and intentional practice. This exercise is designed to be completed in about 10–15 minutes. Trust your first honest answers. You will also find a rundown conclusion that highlights the main ideas of those sections again for easier reference called **Key Insights**. It is made for a quick skim of the chapter without having to read everything again.

Throughout this book, we'll explore everything I've learned—from lessons in uniform to failures in business to building discipline to finding faith again. Stories, frameworks, and examples show the evolution of PRS and how it works in daily life. You'll meet the quadrant behavioral model (quadrant model) that shows where you stand and the AAAA (4A Framework) that will help you move forward. Plus, learning how to apply practical tools like SMART goals and SWOT analysis will help you stay on track and make smarter, values-driven decisions.

The book was further inspired and patterned after *Atomic Habits* by James Clear and *The Subtle Art of Not Giving a F*ck* by Mark Manson. It touches on important elements from both books, such as the importance of mindset and attitude from Mark's book and aspects of the tools and techniques from James's work. These books are great on their own, but they were missing something; a system, framework, and a model to bring everything together. Hence PRS was born.

Before we dive into the system itself, I want you to remember one truth that runs through every page of this book. Everything in life moves. Whether forward or backward, fast or slow, intentionally or not, we are always in motion and that defines our progress, growth, and even failure. Later, we'll explore this concept through Newton's Laws of Motion and how those principles can also govern the way we think, act, and grow. Once you understand motion, you'll understand how the PRS system helps you control it, direct it, balance it and turn it into momentum.

Every great journey needs a roadmap. A way to see not just where you're headed, but how each part of the journey connects. The PRS system provides that structure. It brings together purpose, identity, mindset, behavior, momentum, decision-making, and maintenance into a single, cohesive approach to problem re-solving.

When these components align, progress stops feeling forced. Action becomes intentional, resistance decreases, and momentum builds on its own. This state is often called *flow*—not something you enter deliberately, but something that emerges when clarity, balance, and momentum are working together.

The graphic shows the flow of the PRS system. It represents the full life cycle of PRS. Starting from setting your goals and objectives to truly mastering transformation. The key layers are **mission**, **motive**, **method**, **mentality**, **model**, **movement**, **mapping**, and **maintenance** with everything culminating in **mastery** of progress. Each component aligns to a layer for the system labeled form; goals and objectives, purpose and identity, system and structure, mindset and attitude, behavior and actions, framework and momentum, approaches and applications, and lastly tools and techniques.

Problem Re-Solving System & Components

FLOW	FORM	FORCE
Mission	Goals & Objectives	Destination
Motive	Purpose & Identity	Driver
Method	System & Structure	Vehicle
Mentality	Mindset & Attitude	Fuel
Model	Behavior & Actions	Dashboard
Movement	Framework & Momentum	Engine
Mapping	Approaches & Applications	Navigation
Maintenance	Tools & Techniques	Tool Kit
	MASTERY	

Illustration 1

To help visualize this into something familiar and see how they are put together and function. Think of a car and a journey. You must have a destination, a driver, a vehicle, fuel, a dashboard, an engine, navigation, and maintenance. Each part has a role in the journey. None work alone. Together, they transform effort into forward motion.

I want to make sure you're ready, not just with information, but with the right mission. The bigger reason behind everything you do. Your ultimate goal. It defines where you are headed and why it matters. You don't have to define this now but keep this in mind throughout the whole journey. You will understand in depth later on with the power of why.

Without preparation, even the best tools will feel overwhelming. This journey begins with your attitude, your awareness, and your willingness to face what's in front of you. Awareness and clarity don't happen overnight, but with the right system, they become repeatable habits for life.

In these pages, I'll share the mindsets, attitudes, tools, and strategies I use every day to overcome problems and stay grounded. I don't claim to have all the answers—but I've built a process that works, and I want to share it with you.

I'm not here to tell you what the right or wrong decision is. Life is too complex for that. What I can do is help you understand the right way to approach decisions—and the wrong way to approach them. The outcome will always be yours. Sometimes decisions will work. Sometimes they won't. But when you move with clarity, intention, and balance, you can stand by your choices—even when they backfire. At least you tried. At least you acted with integrity. In the end, you can't make everyone happy. And you're not supposed to. The goal isn't approval—it's alignment.

And finally, a note of transparency. In writing this book, I used every tool I could find—articles, research, mentors, interviews, and yes, even AI—to help organize ideas and refine thoughts. But every story, model, and framework comes from lived experience. These pages are the product of trial, error, and hard-earned wisdom.

Know that no matter where you are or what you're facing, you're not alone. You don't have to stay stuck. You can build balance, create momentum, and design a better path forward. Whether you're a professional in transition, a student figuring out life, a parent juggling priority, or simply someone ready to stop feeling stuck, moving forward is not about solving every problem perfectly. It's about learning how to handle whatever comes next. Think of PRS like a recipe. It's both a science and an art. Science gives you structure; art lets you make it your own. Over time, as you practice the principles, you'll find your rhythm. You'll make fewer mistakes, and when you do, you'll recover faster. This book is my way of paying forward what life, failure, and persistence have taught me. Let's begin.

Goals & Objectives

"If you don't know where you are going,
you'll end up someplace else."
Yogi Berra

Before solving any problem, we must first understand why we are moving at all. Every journey, whether personal or professional, always begins with a destination. Without one, effort becomes motion without meaning, and action turns into reaction. Basically, we go nowhere or just go in circles. Remember, the PRS system follows a deliberate flow — mission, motive, method, mindset, model, movement, mapping, and maintenance. Each chapter builds on the last, revealing a deeper layer of how problems are understood, re-solved, and sustained over time.

In this chapter, we will define and establish the first and most foundational element of the PRS, **mission**, because clarity of direction must come before clarity of self.

- Mission represents your goals and objectives or as a destination— the bigger reason behind everything you do. It defines where you're headed, why that direction matters, and what success actually looks like to you. Without mission, even the best tools, strategies, and frameworks eventually stall.

Mission is not about lofty slogans or vague aspirations. When you know your destination, decisions become easier, priorities sharpen, and problems stop feeling random. Mission gives context to struggle and meaning to effort. It turns chaos into a journey with intent.

The Power of Why

"People don't buy what you do; they buy why you do it."
Simon Sinek

One of the most powerful concepts in personal and professional growth comes from Simon Sinek's bestselling book *Start With Why*. Having all the solutions to everything does not matter if there is no "Why" in the equation. His work reinforces a truth that sits at the heart of PRS, that purpose must come before process. We will go over purpose in depth in the next chapter, but it needs to be established here.

According to Simon, successful individuals and organizations begin with a clear sense of purpose, their Why, rather than focusing solely on what they do or how they do it. This deeper purpose becomes a guiding force that shapes decisions, actions, and direction. Sinek's Golden Circle model comprises three layers:

- **Why** – The purpose, cause, or belief that drives you.
- **How** – The process or approach you take to bring your Why to life.
- **What** – The result or outcome of your actions (e.g., your job, your role, your product).

Most people and organizations operate from the outside in (What → How → Why), but the most effective leaders and change makers operate from the inside out (Why → How → What). Instead of focusing on what to do and how to do it, with why being last, it should be reversed. The why should come first. It's what remains when motivation fades, setbacks pile up, or progress feels slow.

Understanding your Why is crucial before engaging in the process of solving problems, addressing challenges, or adapting to change in any area of your life. Your Why becomes your anchor, your fuel, and your compass, making it easier to stay focused, take action, and endure setbacks. Choose something that aligns with your strengths, passions, and the needs of the world. This gives everything you do, meaning, and motivation. This concept fits hand-in-hand with everything we're building in this book. If you're lost, unmotivated, or stuck in inaction, chances are you've lost connection with your why. In PRS, your Why becomes your reference point. When faced with uncertainty, it answers questions like:

- Is this problem worth solving?
- Is this obstacle aligned with where I'm trying to go?
- Should I push through, pivot, or pause?

Without a Why, hesitation grows. With one, clarity returns. Your Why eventually becomes something deeper than motivation. It becomes trust. Not religious faith — but belief in something higher than the moment you're in. Confidence that your effort matters, even when results aren't immediate. Assurance that staying aligned is more important than reacting to every setback.

Think about something as simple as tomorrow morning. You don't wake up and question whether the sun will rise. You trust it will — not because you proved it, but because experience, pattern, and consistency have earned that trust. Your Why works the same way. When progress is slow, energy is low, and doubt creeps in, your Why becomes the thing you trust to carry you forward. Your Why doesn't need to be dramatic or grand. It must be strong. It must be something you can explain, defend, and return to when life tries to shake you. Because if you don't trust your Why, you'll abandon it the moment things get uncomfortable.

Your Why represents the ultimate direction of your life. All other goals and accomplishments support it, not replace it. They act as stepping stones — small, measurable points of progress that move you closer to what truly matters. Checklists and task completion help you stay organized, but your Why gives those efforts meaning. Without it, you may stay busy without ever feeling fulfilled.

Before you define your own Why, it helps to see what a strong, defensible Why looks like in real life. As a first-generation immigrant born into poverty, my Why is rooted in legacy. I want to build something meaningful that outlives me — for my children, my grandchildren, and the generations that come after. That purpose keeps me moving even when the tank is empty and my tires feel worn down. It's why I continue to work, dream, and build despite setbacks. My family and the legacy I leave behind — both tangible and intangible, from stability and opportunity to values, lessons, and memories — are what anchor me. That is my Why. What is yours?

If you're struggling to write your Why, don't start with what you want to become. Start with what you're afraid of becoming—or afraid of losing. Fear often reveals what matters most. When named honestly, it can be transformed from a limiting force into a guiding one. Fear is not meant to be your permanent motivator. This is only a starting point. As clarity grows, your Why should evolve from fear-avoidance into purpose-creation.

When your mission aligns with who you are and what you value, problems stop feeling like barriers and start becoming part of the path. So, before moving forward, ask yourself this question: What destination am I truly moving toward—and why does it matter to me?

Define Your Mission

"Clarity doesn't come from answers.
It comes from choosing a direction."

This exercise takes 10–15 minutes. Don't overthink it. Before you try to fix problems, change habits, or build momentum, you need a clear destination. This exercise is not about perfection—it's about direction. Your mission can evolve, but it must exist. Take a few quiet minutes and answer the following honestly.

Step 1: Clarify Your Destination. Answer each question in one or two sentences—no overthinking.

- What area of your life feels most important to improve right now? (Career, health, relationships, finances, purpose, balance, etc.)
- If things were working the way you hoped in this area, what would "better" actually look like?
- What am I afraid of or what will I be losing?

Example: I want financial freedom to build stability so my family never experiences the uncertainty I did. Or I'm afraid I'll struggle financially my entire life.

Step 2: Identify Your Why. This is not about what sounds impressive—this is about what feels true. Your Why is not meant to inspire you once. It's meant to carry you repeatedly — especially when motivation disappears. Ask yourself:

- Why does this goal matter to me personally?
- What pain am I trying to move away from?
- What future am I trying to move toward?

If this goal disappeared tomorrow, what would I lose? Write freely. One paragraph is enough.

Step 3: Define Your Why. Using what you wrote above, complete this sentence:

I want to ____

because ____.

Keep it short. You should be able to remember it without notes. Write what feels true right now. This exercise will help you move beyond surface-level goals and uncover a Why that is defensible, durable, and trusted.

Step 4: Apply the Trust Test. A strong Why provides clarity, not stress. Now challenge your Why by asking the following questions:

- Would this Why still matter if progress took twice as long?
- Would it still matter if no one noticed or praised you?
- Would it still matter if the results were uncertain or delayed?
- Would I still pursue this if the path became uncomfortable?

If your Why collapses under these questions, it's not wrong — it's just not fully formed yet. You'll revisit and refine this Why later. For now, you're simply testing whether it can support forward movement.

KEY INSIGHTS FOR CHAPTER 1

- **Mission is not motivation—it's direction**. When your goals and objectives are clear, decision-making becomes simpler, more intentional, and less reactive.

- **Clarity does not require certainty**. Choosing a direction—even an imperfect one—creates momentum. Mission is a starting reference point, not a final destination.

- **Motivation fades. Trust remains**. A strong Why isn't loud or emotional—it's reliable. Trust carries you forward when progress is slow, uncertain, or uncomfortable.

- **Starting with Why is a foundational PRS tool**. It anchors your actions in purpose and transforms uncertainty into forward movement rather than hesitation.

- **If defining your Why felt difficult, that's information—not failure**. Resistance often signals misalignment or lack of clarity, not a lack of capability.

- **A defensible Why simplifies decisions**. When your Why can survive delay, discomfort, or lack of recognition, it becomes easier to decide whether to push forward, pivot, or pause.

- **When you feel stuck, overwhelmed, or disengaged, the issue is often not effort or skill—it's an unclear or disconnected mission**. Reconnecting to your Why restores context and direction.

- **Mission is meant to be used, not perfected**. You will revisit and refine it over time. For now, it exists to guide action and reduce friction.
- **Before planning your next steps, return to your Why**. It may be the one thing that transforms hesitation into momentum—and problems into progress.

Purpose & Identity

"He who has a Why to live can bear almost any How."
Friedrich Nietzsche

The first chapter established mission—your destination and direction. But direction alone doesn't move you. Many people know where they want to go and remain stuck. The missing element is **motive** which turns direction into movement. In the PRS system, motive follows mission intentionally. Who are you while pursuing it?

- Motive is your purpose and identity as a driver in motion. It's the internal alignment between who you are and what drives you, the inner urgency that fuels you to take action, even when the road feels uncertain.

This chapter is about purpose and identity—and how the two are inseparable. Motive isn't motivation. Motivation is emotional. It comes and goes. It spikes and crashes. Motive is deeper than that. Motive is the internal alignment between who you are and what you're pursuing. It's the quiet pressure that keeps you moving when excitement fades, when progress slows, or when no one is watching. Your identity—how you see yourself, what you value, what feels natural versus forced—shapes how you respond to problems long before logic kicks in. When your goals line up with your identity, action feels honest. It feels sustainable. So, you don't have to convince yourself every day to keep going.

When goals don't align with identity, everything feels heavy. Progress becomes a show rather than genuine achievement. Discipline starts to feel like punishment. That's usually when burnout shows up. Most people don't quit because they're weak. They quit because they're fighting themselves.

Identity shapes how you interpret stress, opportunity, and uncertainty—what you avoid, what you over-commit to, and what you tell yourself when things don't go as planned. Most people don't struggle because they lack motivation—they struggle because they don't recognize how their identity is influencing their choices in the moment.

Identity Matters

"Be yourself; everyone else is already taken."
Oscar Wilde

Your identity doesn't start forming when you write goals down in a notebook. It starts much earlier—often before you have language for it.

If you grew up family-first, loyalty and responsibility are probably baked into you. If you had to survive early, adapt quickly, or help provide, efficiency and urgency may drive you. If humor helps you cope, you may process stress through levity. If structure gives you safety, you may thrive with routines and systems. If independence was forced on you, autonomy might matter more than recognition.

None of this is good or bad. It is what it is. Problems show up when people try to adopt identities that aren't theirs. You can feel it immediately when someone is pretending—trying to be loud when they're quiet, aggressive when they're reflective, funny when they're not. Nothing drains energy faster than performing an identity that doesn't fit. PRS doesn't ask you to reinvent yourself. It asks you to be honest about who you already are—and then build from there.

Purpose doesn't come from copying someone else's blueprint. It comes from alignment—when your experiences, values, and identity point in the same direction. When goals reflect who you are, progress feels meaningful. Discipline feels natural. Consistency replaces force.

When goals fight your identity, motivation fades quickly. Resistance shows up as procrastination or burnout. Progress feels like self-betrayal. This is why PRS treats motive as identity in motion. Your why isn't a slogan or a sentence you memorize. It's a reflection of how you're wired—and how you move when pressure shows up.

Identity is not a label you choose once—it's a pattern that reveals itself under pressure. When decisions feel heavy, motivation fades, or fear shows up, your identity doesn't disappear. It speaks louder. PRS doesn't ask you to change who you are—it teaches you how to recognize who's showing up and respond with intention.

Why PRS Exists

"Efforts and courage are not enough without purpose and direction."
John F. Kennedy

I didn't learn problem-solving from books. I learned it from survival. Being born into poverty and living in a third world country determined a lot about me. Growing up in scarcity shapes you, whether or not you realize it. Efficiency isn't optional. Adaptation isn't philosophical—it's required. When resources are limited, you learn quickly that not all problems are the same. Some demand immediate action. Some require patience. Others can't be solved at all and must be navigated instead.

That environment didn't just shape my circumstances—it shaped my instincts. The need to anticipate., conserve energy, and move with intention. When I later faced new systems, new pressures, and new responsibilities, that identity followed me. Over time, one pattern became impossible to ignore: motion without alignment leads to burnout. I was working hard. I was solving problems. But I wasn't moving sustainably. I was reacting more than choosing.

PRS didn't come from theory—it came from reflection. From recognizing patterns. From learning that progress requires more than effort. It requires clarity about who you are and why you move the way you do. My story isn't the point of this chapter. It's the proof.

This chapter is about helping you understand why you move the way you do. Before you refine strategies, tools, or habits, you need to answer one foundational question. Am I building a future that fits who I am—or am I fighting myself to get there? When motive and identity align, effort multiplies instead of draining. When they don't, no system will save you. PRS starts here—not with pressure, but with honesty.

Now that you've clarified your mission and you're beginning to understand your identity, something important happens: movement becomes possible—but also dangerous without structure. Many people reach this point and assume the next step is to just take action. They work harder. Push faster. Add more effort. But effort without structure doesn't lead to progress—it leads to burnout.

PRS exists because problems don't just test our plans—they test who we believe we are. Learning to recognize that moment turns reaction into intention. Purpose gives you direction. Identity determines how you move when the path gets difficult.

Throughout this book, you'll see the same problem approached in different ways—not because the situation changed, but because the person facing it did. As you move into the next chapters, pay attention to how your identity shows up under pressure. Awareness here will make every tool, model, and framework more effective later.

Identify Your Motive

"Clarity begins when you stop guessing and start understanding yourself."

This short reflection is designed to help you surface patterns, not solve them, and will take 10–15 minutes. Don't overthink it. You're not trying to solve your entire life here—you're building awareness. Before you change how you act, you need to understand who is acting. Understanding your motive doesn't require answers—it requires honesty.

Step 1: Identify Your Default Driver (2–3 minutes). Write a few sentences. There's no right answer—only awareness. Answer honestly:

- When pressure increases, do you push harder, avoid, analyze, or react quickly?
- When things go wrong, what do you usually rely on—discipline, speed, reflection, control, or endurance?

Step 2: Reflect on the Origin (4–5 minutes). Now ask yourself where this pattern came from. One short paragraph is enough. This isn't about blame. It's about context.

- What experiences shaped how you deal with problems?
- What did you learn about survival, success, or safety early in life?
- What traits helped you endure—but may now create friction?

Step 3: Name the Identity at Work (2–3 minutes). This is not who you want to be—it's who currently shows up. Naming it doesn't lock you in—it gives you leverage. Complete this sentence honestly:

- When faced with difficulty, I see myself as someone who

  _________________________.

Step 4: Alignment Check (3–4 minutes). If the answer feels unclear, that's okay. Awareness comes before change. You'll revisit and refine identity later. For now, you're simply noticing the driver behind your motion. Ask yourself:

- Does this identity support my mission—or sabotage it?
- Does it help me move forward sustainably, or only in short bursts?
- Is this response intentional—or reactive?

KEY INSIGHTS FOR CHAPTER 2

- **Mission defines where you're going.** Motive determines whether you can sustain the journey.

- **Your identity shapes how you respond under pressure.** Conscious or not, it influences decisions, habits, and reactions.

- **Motion without awareness leads to burnout.** Effort alone creates cycles. Awareness creates progress.

- **Your motive existed before you named it.** Life experiences—especially hardship—quietly shape how you solve problems.

- **Not all problems require the same response.** Some demand action, others reflection, and some require adaptation. Awareness reveals the difference.

- **Experience becomes useful only when reflected upon.** Reflection turns history into insight—and insight into a tool.

- **Your journey shaped you in ways you're still discovering.** When reflected upon, experience becomes insight, and insight becomes a tool for growth.

- **PRS does not begin with tools or techniques.** It begins with purpose and identity.

- **You don't need to change your identity yet.** Recognizing it is the first act of intentional movement.

- **Your past doesn't define you—but it shapes you.** When understood, it becomes an advantage instead of a weight.

System & Structure

"You do not rise to the level of your goals.
You fall to the level of your systems."
James Clear

The first two chapters established your foundation. In Chapter 1, you defined your mission—where you're going. In Chapter 2, you clarified your motive—who you are while going there and why it matters. But clarity alone does not create progress.

Many people know what they want. Many understand why it matters. Yet they still feel stuck, overwhelmed, or burned out. Purpose without a system or structure leads to frustration. Identity without a method leads to inconsistency. What's missing is method. Method is not motivation. It's not willpower. It's not doing more. In this chapter we will cover:

- Method is the system and structure within PRS that acts as your vehicle—turning mission and motive into intentional, repeatable movement.

Method is how intention becomes execution. It's the system and structure that turns your mission and motive into consistent movement. In the PRS System, method functions as your vehicle—the practical foundation that carries you forward in a way that's repeatable, sustainable, and aligned.

In PRS, method is not a single technique or a checklist you complete once and move on from. It is the repeatable structure you return to whenever life presents a problem, a challenge, or a major change.

Without method, effort becomes reactive. You respond based on urgency, emotion, or habit. With method, action becomes deliberate. You slow the moment down just enough to choose your next move instead of defaulting to old patterns.

Mission defines where you're going. Motive fuels the desire to move. Method determines how you move—especially when things aren't clear, calm, or convenient. PRS is built on the idea that most problems aren't solved once. They're re-solved over time. Method is what makes that possible.

In this chapter, you'll learn how to use a method that supports your goals without overwhelming you—so progress becomes something you can sustain, not something you constantly struggle to maintain.

The PRS System

"Never try to solve all the problems at once — make them line up for you one-by-one."
Richard Sloma

When I first began building it, I didn't want another complicated model that looked good on paper but fell apart in real life. I needed something that could actually help people think better, act smarter, and move with clarity when life gets messy. So, whether you're frozen by fear, overthinking, acting without a plan, or already on the right path, the PRS system is a simple structure that helps you figure out where you are mentally and what actions you need to take next for navigating problems, challenges, and change. It's built on eight interconnected components that work together like a living, breathing system — each with a unique role, yet all dependent on one another to create clarity, balance, and forward motion.

And you can always come back to it when life throws something hard your way—relationship issues, career decisions, financial stress, or moments when you feel overwhelmed. That's exactly what the PRS system was designed to do.

Before you get into the behavioral and mechanical parts of the PRS System, you need to ground yourself in your purpose. Every journey begins with direction, identity, and a plan to move forward. These three foundational components — **mission, motive,** and **method** — form the base of your system. They define why you're moving, who you are, and how you intend to get there. When your motive and identity align, your drive becomes unstoppable. Your method is your structure — the practical roadmap that turns your mission and motive into movement.

It's the system you use to translate purpose into planning, giving your effort form and direction instead of chaos and reaction.

These three components work quietly beneath everything else in the PRS. You won't find them labeled in every exercise or framework, but they're always there — implied, guiding, and shaping your approach. Together, they ensure that every choice, plan, and action connects back to meaning, identity, and direction. Once your mission, motive, and method are clear, the rest of the PRS comes alive. That's when mindset, models, and momentum can truly do their work — helping you move forward with purpose and balance.

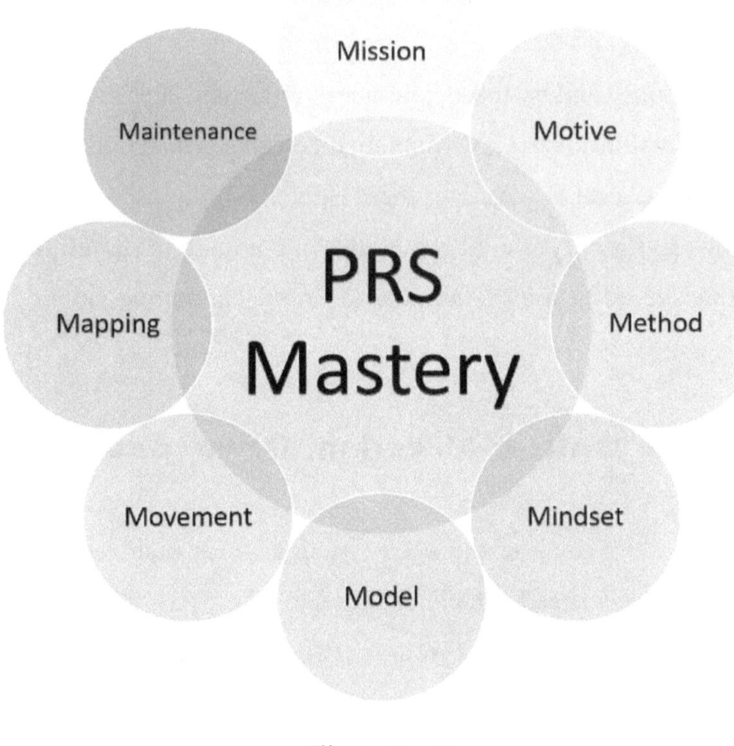

Illustration 2

Then comes your **mentality**, the emotional and psychological core that fuels everything else. It's the combination of attitude, belief, and discipline that powers the system — your internal fuel and battery. Without it, nothing moves. At the center sits your **model** — the PRS quadrant model that reveals your behavioral patterns: when you hesitate, overthink, act impulsively, or move with balance. Awareness of your current quadrant helps you correct course before repeating the same mistakes. Next is **movement**, powered by the 4A Framework. This enables you to keep moving intentionally and take advantage of the small wins. Then comes **mapping** — your decision-making approaches that keep you aligned and adaptive, such as the 5 Why's or the Yes-or-No Philosophy. Mapping ensures that when obstacles appear, you can reroute effectively instead of losing direction. Finally, we have **maintenance** — your daily tools and techniques. These are the tangible actions that keep everything tuned and balanced: journaling, reflection, checklists, trackers, and accountability systems. Maintenance transforms good intentions into sustained results. Together, these eight components form the PRS.

Now, to simplify it a bit more we can compare to something that everyone should be a bit familiar with simple car components.

PRS as a Vehicle: Direction, Drive, and Control

You can also think of the PRS system as a car built for your life's journey—a finely tuned vehicle designed to take you from confusion to clarity, from reaction to results. Your mission is the **destination**—the place you ultimately want to reach. It's your vision of success, the coordinates that guide every move you make. Your motive is the **driver**. It's your purpose and identity—the reason you get behind the wheel in the first place. Without motive, the car may exist, but it will not go anywhere. Your method is the **vehicle** itself. It's the structure, design, and system that connects all the moving parts of the PRS. A good vehicle doesn't just look good—it's engineered for endurance, performance, and purpose. Your mindset is the **fuel and battery** that powers everything. Without the right mindset and attitude, the engine won't start, and momentum stalls before it begins. The quadrant behavioral model is your **dashboard**, and it helps you understand how you're driving, where you're drifting, and when to adjust your course. It's awareness in motion. Your momentum—powered by the 4A Framework—is the **engine**. It converts energy into action through four stages of continuous motion. This keeps you moving forward. Mapping represents your **navigation** system; think of it as the GPS that keeps you aligned, helping you reroute when life throws a detour. With mapping, even wrong turns lead to lessons and better direction. And finally, your maintenance tools are your tune-up **toolkit**: journaling, reflection, trackers, and routines keep your vehicle running smoothly for the long haul. Those tools turn momentum into mastery.

PRS & Car Components

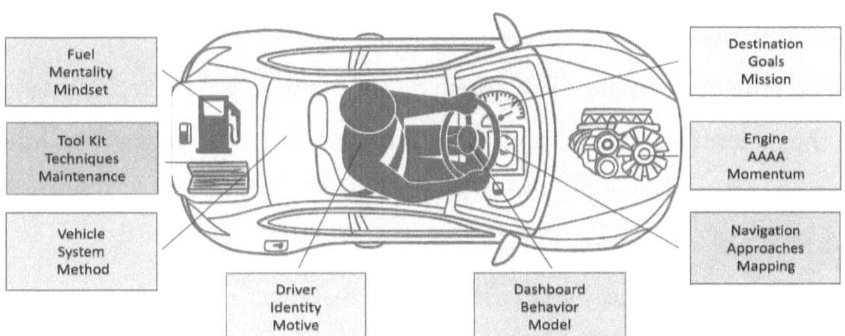

Illustration 3

Together, these eight components form the full PRS system—a self-sustaining machine built for growth, resilience, and clarity. It's not about doing more; it's about knowing how you move, why you move, and where you're headed.

The PRS Cycle

Most traditional problem-solving models follow a logical, linear sequence. You define the problem, analyze the cause, implement a solution, and evaluate the result. These approaches work well in controlled environments—business processes, manufacturing systems, or technical workflows. Life is rarely that controlled.

Most models assume clear thinking, emotional neutrality, stable conditions, and one-time solutions. PRS assumes the opposite. It assumes that people make emotional decisions first and justify them later. It assumes clarity is often missing at the start. It assumes momentum fluctuates. And it assumes that unresolved patterns tend to repeat themselves in new forms. That's why PRS focuses on problem re-solving, not one-time problem solving. It's designed for real life, where pressure, uncertainty, and repetition are normal.

At the heart of the PRS system method is the PRS cycle. This cycle is the general way PRS approaches any problem, challenge, or change. It's intentionally simple, because clarity should not feel complicated when life already does.

The PRS cycle moves through five stages: **recognize, clarify, choose, move, and recalibrate.** You begin by recognizing what's really bothering you. This isn't about perfect language—it's about honesty. If you can't name the issue, you can't move it.

From there, you clarify what's happening. This is where awareness comes in. You pause long enough to understand your thoughts, emotions, and current position before acting. Most people skip this step and wonder why they keep repeating the same problems.

Next, you choose a direction. Not the perfect answer. Not the full plan. Just the next right move. Then you move. Progress begins with action, not certainty. The goal is forward motion that's balanced and intentional, not rushed or forced.

Finally, you recalibrate. You reflect, adjust, and re-solve. Growth is not a straight line—it's a loop. Each pass through the cycle sharpens your judgment and strengthens your momentum. This cycle is the method.

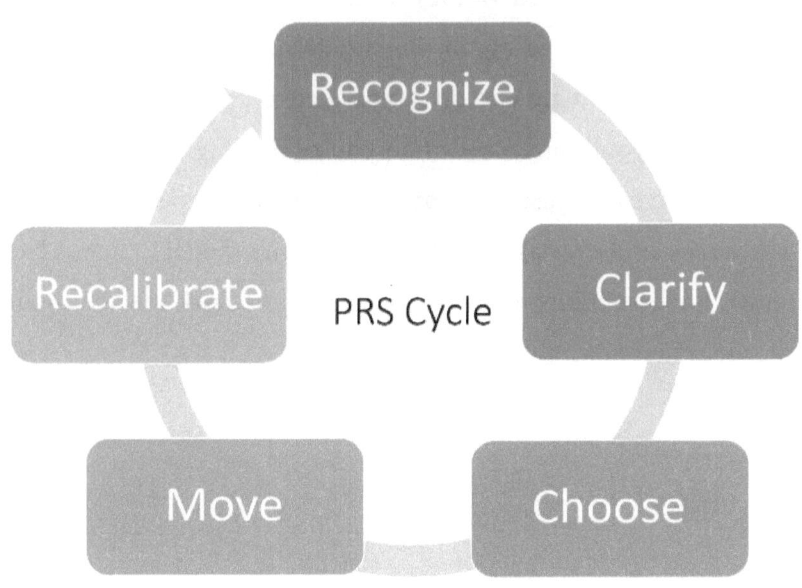

Illustration 4

The PRS Behavioral Quadrant Model

Most people don't fail because they lack solutions. They fail because they act before they understand what's really happening. PRS intentionally slows you down at the point of clarity. PRS includes a behavioral quadrant model to support awareness and clarity.

The model helps you recognize how you're approaching a problem before you act. At different times, you may find yourself avoiding, overthinking, acting impulsively, or moving with balance. The quadrant model doesn't label you. It orients you. It reveals patterns so you can adjust before repeating them. Awareness in PRS isn't abstract—it's observable and actionable.

The quadrant model highlights four common problem-solving patterns: the **Fearful Avoider**, the **Reflective Thinker**, the **Impulsive Actor**, and the **Balanced Achiever**. Each one represents a mindset we can fall into, depending on the situation. This model helps you recognize where you are and gives you a clear path forward. It helps you recognize your patterns—when you're holding back, or rushing ahead—so you can adjust your approach instead of repeating the same mistakes over and over again. We'll explore the model in depth later. For now, understand its role: it helps you see yourself clearly enough to choose differently.

PRS Behavioral Quadrant Model

Illustration 5

I've used the quadrant model to survive and grow through real life. I have been all four personas in one or several of my problems. Some problems I was able to solve as one persona most often I had to mentally shift between them to overcome obstacles and setbacks. But that's the key awareness and the strive to keep moving.

PRS 4A Framework

Many systems focus on finding the "right" answer. PRS focuses on staying in motion without tipping into extremes. Balance prevents paralysis and burnout. Momentum prevents stagnation and false starts. PRS doesn't rush decisions, but it also doesn't reward hesitation. It teaches you how to move steadily, adjust intelligently, and keep going even when conditions aren't ideal. This is where PRS differs most from traditional approaches. It's not about intensity—it's about continuity.

PRS supports momentum through the **4A Framework**: **anticipate**, **activate**, **advance**, and **achieve**. The framework operates inside the **move** stage of the PRS Cycle. It governs how momentum unfolds once action begins, ensuring progress doesn't stall or spiral.

Anticipate is the stage that gets you physically, mentally, and spiritually ready. It's the planning and preparing for the journey of problem re-solving. Activate is the conscious decision to start addressing the situation with clarity. Seeing how you start approaching problems and awareness of how you act and respond. Advance is staying balanced and starting and keeping momentum going. Achieve is the final stage and phase for reflection and lessons learned and gets you ready for the next scenario. Please note Anticipate is a core function and should always be performed; utilizing this will resolve your problems, challenges, and changes effectively and efficiently.

PRS 4A Framework

Illustration 6

The 4A Framework is the core component for movement and momentum. We'll break this framework down in detail later. For now, know this: PRS builds momentum by design, not by motivation alone. To bring it all together. The PRS system shows you the components at play. The PRS cycle tells you what phase you're in. The quadrant model reveals how you're showing up. And the 4A Framework shows you how to keep moving. That integration is what separates PRS from traditional problem-solving models.

My work in cyber security and the Risk Management Framework created by the National Institute of Standards and Technology inspired the creation of this framework. Even though these were specifically geared towards IT, I tailored them to help me find balance, build momentum, and survive and grow in my life.

Just recently, I used this whole system for one of my clients. We were in a high-pressure project, and the process was chaotic. Deadlines overlapped, people were reactive, and we were all basically cyber firefighters. I realized we needed to get the team grounded. So, I paused, reflected, and applied the PRS system. I prepared the team for the scope, schedule, and requirements, which helped us anticipate real-world issues like communication and collaboration gaps. Everything was easier once we assigned priorities and had everyone working in unison towards the project plan and schedule which was crucial with our multi-department team. Think of multiple fire departments, coordinating to put out the California wildfires stretched across hundreds of thousands of acres each with their own areas to control and obstacles to face but with the same singular goal. We completed the project on time and more effectively.

Establishing PRS

"A clear system removes confusion and preserves energy."

This exercise helps you establish method, not solve everything at once. The goal is to create enough structure to move forward without overwhelm. You are not building a perfect plan — you are building a usable system you can return to when life becomes messy.

Set aside 10–15 minutes. Keep your answers simple. Method works best when it's lightweight and repeatable.

Step 1: Identify the Problem You're Actually Solving (2–3 minutes). Choose one problem, challenge, or area of friction you're dealing with right now. Answer briefly:

- What situation am I trying to move forward right now?
- What would *progress* look like — not perfection?

Step 2: Externalize the Moving Parts (3–4 minutes). Overwhelm usually comes from trying to manage complexity mentally. Get it out of your head and onto the page. List anything related to this issue:

- Tasks
- Decisions
- People involved
- Constraints
- Unknowns

Don't organize yet. Just unload.

Step 3: Apply Simple Structure (3–4 minutes). Now introduce light order:

- Circle what must happen first.
- Cross out what does not need attention right now
- Highlight one action that would move things forward today

Your goal is not completion. Your goal is sequence.

Step 4: Define PRS Statement (2–3 minutes). This step anchors PRS as your **system**, not just a concept. Complete this sentence:

Using the **PRS** system, my current approach to this issue is to

____.

Example: Using the PRS system, my current approach to this issue is to slow the situation down, clarify whether I'm dealing with a problem, challenge, or change, take one intentional step forward instead of reacting, and adjust based on what happens next.

Keep it practical and realistic. It's a reference point you can return to and refine as you move forward.

Step 5: Check for Alignment (2–3 minutes). Ask yourself:

- Does this method support my mission?
- Does it fit who I am and how I operate?
- Does it reduce confusion or add to it?

If it feels heavy, simplify. Method should support motion, not slow it down.

Before You Move On. You are not locking yourself into anything. You are creating structure for the next stretch of road. That's what method is for. If this exercise felt easier or harder than expected, pay attention. How you responded matters—and we'll explore why in the next chapter.

KEY INSIGHTS FOR CHAPTER 3

- **Mission defines where you're going.** It provides direction and meaning so effort isn't wasted.

- **Motive explains who is moving.** It reflects your purpose, identity, and internal driver under pressure.

- **Method is how you move.** PRS itself is the system and structure that turns clarity into action.

- **Mentality fuels movement.** Your mindset and attitude determine whether structure creates momentum or resistance.

- **Model provides awareness.** The PRS Quadrant Model shows how you're responding in real time.

- **Movement builds momentum.** The 4A Framework explains how progress unfolds through intentional motion.

- **Mapping supports decisions.** It helps you adapt and reroute without panic or overcorrection.

- **Maintenance sustains progress.** Daily tools and practices keep balance and prevent burnout.

- **When all eight components align, you move in harmony with the same laws that govern the universe: inertia, acceleration, and action-reaction.** You're no longer fighting motion—you're mastering it, transforming every challenge into purposeful forward momentum.

- **The PRS Cycle (recognize, clarify, choose, move, recalibrate) provides a usable structure for real-life complexity.** It keeps you from reacting blindly and gives you a repeatable way to regain clarity when situations change.

- **Awareness must come before action if progress is going to last.** The quadrant model helps you see how you're approaching a situation before you act.

- **Momentum is not created by intensity or urgency.** It's built through continuity—small, intentional actions repeated with awareness over time.

- **The 4A Framework governs how movement unfolds once action begins.** It helps you stay in motion without tipping into burnout, paralysis, or chaotic overcorrection.

- **Overwhelm decreases when structure replaces reaction.** By slowing down, externalizing the moving parts, and sequencing one intentional step, you experienced how clarity restores momentum without force.

Mindset & Attitude

"You cannot solve a problem with the same mind that created it."
Albert Einstein

Our ancestors faced survival we face distraction. But in every generation, the skill to recognize and resolve problems remains, the key to progress. We know life is full of problems — big or small, obvious or hidden, personal or professional. We all face moments that demand action, patience, or change. You might be stressed about not getting enough likes on social media, or you might be worried about how to pay your next bill. In both cases, you have a problem, even if the scale differs from those faced by our ancestors. And if you've ever felt like life just keeps throwing one challenge at you after another, you're not alone. But here's the thing, problems are nothing new. In fact, they've been part of the human story from the very beginning.

It's easy to look back and say that past generations dealt with harder lives. In many ways, they did. Early humans struggled with basic survival, such as hunting for food, protecting their families from wild animals or rival tribes, building shelter, and enduring harsh weather without modern medicine or conveniences. Today, we've traded many of those challenges for ones of complexity, speed, and noise. We no longer fear the winter's chill in a cave, but we do fear missing a mortgage payment, losing a job, piled-up emails, or not living up to expectations. These might seem life-threatening, but they still weigh heavily on us. Problems haven't disappeared. They've simply evolved.

That's why this chapter matters. Complaining or avoiding problems isn't what matters. It's about preparing and anticipating. Recognizing that every difficulty calls for a specific approach is key—whether you're in a flooded street in Cavite or sitting in a cubicle facing burnout—demands a specific approach.

This chapter is about getting your mind right before the real work begins. Before you can make lasting change or fix real problems, you need to understand what you're up against. That means breaking down the difference between a problem, a challenge, and a change, because not all adversity is created equal.

We'll also explore how your mentality affects your response. If fear, procrastination, or being overwhelmed is holding you back, we'll talk about why and what to do about it. We'll take lessons from others, explore what balance really means, and show you how to take ownership of your situation, even if it wasn't your fault.

That's why this chapter and this book exist. My goal is to help you prepare for life's many problems, challenges, and changes. Not just by reacting to them, but by understanding them and choosing the best strategy to deal with them. Here's what you can expect in this chapter:

- Mentality is your mindset and attitude is your fuel and battery — it powers your internal energy, discipline, and emotional readiness and drive to keep going when challenges arise.
- Define the differences between your problems, challenges, and changes.
- Gain awareness and clarity to start PRS.
- Unpack the common mindsets that hold us back.
- Explore how to shift your thinking from fear to action.
- The foundational balance of the Three-Legged Stool of physical, mental, and spiritual strength.
- Develop resilience and persistence.
- Harness the power of attitude, ownership, and reflection.
- Learn how to create balance and build momentum.

So, if you've been stuck, overwhelmed, or unsure of where to begin—this is your starting point. Let's begin with the most powerful step of all: understanding what you're really facing and getting ready to face it. This isn't just about learning definitions. It's about giving you the tools to step into a new way of living and where you face your problems, embrace challenges, and use change as fuel instead of fear. Let's begin.

What Is a Problem?

"It's not a problem that we have a problem. It's a problem
if we don't deal with the problem."
Mary Kay Utech

Big Three Problems, Challenges, & Change

CATEGORY	SUBCATEGORIES	EXAMPLES OF PROBLEMS	EXAMPLES OF CHALLENGES	EXAMPLES OF CHANGES
Financial	Income | Investments | Debt	Debt, lack of savings, unexpected expenses, inflation, poor financial literacy	Balancing budget, saving for retirement, affording housing, managing investments	Marriage/divorce affecting finances, inheritance, sudden windfall or loss
Professional	Job | Career | School & Training	Job loss, stalled growth, skill gaps, workplace conflict, starting a business	Adapting to new leadership, career change, meeting performance goals, work-life balance	Promotion/demotion, relocation for work, starting school or returning to school
Personal	Physical | Mental & Emotional | Spiritual	Chronic illness, anxiety, grief, lack of purpose, strained relationships	Maintaining health, managing stress, nurturing relationships, staying true to values	Parenthood, aging, spiritual awakening, moving to a new place

Illustration 7

Life is full of obstacles. Some we see coming, while others catch us off guard. **Problems, challenges**, and **changes** are an inevitable part of our journey, but they are not all the same. Problems cause stress, difficulty, or uncertainty and require a solution. Challenges are something new and difficult that test our resilience and determination. Changes are shifts in the usual way of doing things. They require adaptation and flexibility. Recognizing these differences is the first step to mastering problem resolution. Here are some common examples we might face in our financial, professional, and personal lives: Coincidentally, it looks like everything that happened in my life with my problems, challenges, and changes. If this were one of those questionnaires that you had to mark one point for everything, I would get the most points in every category.

I believe problems, challenges, and change don't show up randomly. Whether you see it as God, the universe, or life itself, they often appear as a form of correction—or refinement—long before we recognize the need for it. They surface when something is out of alignment, even if we don't yet have the awareness to see it clearly.

Think about how the body works. Many diseases don't present symptoms until much later, not because nothing was wrong, but because the body was compensating for as long as it could. Eventually, the symptoms force attention. They demand correction. Ignoring them isn't an option anymore.

Life works the same way. Problems aren't always punishments—they're signals. Challenges aren't obstacles meant to stop us—they're pressure meant to strengthen us. And change often arrives not when it's convenient, but when it's necessary. PRS exists to help you recognize those signals earlier, respond with clarity instead of panic, and use what shows up—not waste it.

Remember, our goal is to be better prepared for anything that may pop up at some point in the form of balance and momentum. Like having savings in the bank in case the car breaks down or an emergency room visit. Staying up to date on job and career skills in case you get fired or decide to get a new job. Exercising and sleeping well in case you get sick. Everyone gets sick, but healthy people bounce back easier and faster than those who are in poor health.

When I first started working in cybersecurity, a challenge and change arose unexpectedly. I got a contract to help with network security. However, in my first two weeks onsite, the main cybersecurity specialist put in their two weeks' notice. Someone had to step up to do the job until a replacement was hired, so I gladly accepted the challenge. It started with a fast-paced training, and everything seemed to be in order. My confidence was high, since I had an expert trainer with me. But when it was just me doing the job, I started doubting everything I learned and what the heck I just signed up for. Maybe I had not asked the right questions or enough of them. I had no idea what I was doing. Some documents were missing, and many of them were wrong. I had to step up to another level. I could not ignore it because my new job was on the line. So, I dug deep, coordinated with the right teams, trained with other cybersecurity personnel on my own, and just kept trucking on. Eventually everything worked out, but it took a lot of effort and coordination to overcome this challenge.

That's what a problem often looks like in real life—it's not always dramatic or obvious. Sometimes, it just pops up and grabs your whole being for your attention. The stress, uncertainty, or difficulty might build slowly or all at once, but the cost of ignoring it can be massive and worse. Let's analyze my big three in the main categories as that lays the foundation on what I want to work on solving or overcoming.

Financially, my major pain point is managing a big family. Everything is bigger and multiplied when it comes to finances—bigger house, bigger meals, bigger transportation, bigger insurance, and, of course, bigger bills. More food, more clothes, more cars, more phones, more everything. This creates a need for daily awareness of what's coming in and what's going out to maintain a balanced budget.

Professionally, I balance a demanding 9-to-5 job with multiple businesses and this book project. Working in technology means the battle space is constantly shifting. What's current today is outdated by tomorrow. We have to keep up with innovation and security. One example is the rapid rise of artificial intelligence. If you're not learning and leveraging AI daily, you're already behind. It doesn't matter what field you're in—AI touches everything we do.

Personally, I wrestle with maintaining my physical, mental, and spiritual health. I often sleep late but try to always wake up on time. Those routine matters—it builds discipline and consistency. I can't always control what time I go to sleep, but I can control when I get up. It's not always easy, but nothing worthwhile ever is. Remembering the phrase the best things in life are worth waiting for keeps me grounded.

On the mental side, I live with ADHD. My memory is shot, so I write everything down—spreadsheets everywhere. One morning, I was late for work and couldn't find my car keys anywhere. The whole family joined the search. Turns out I had put them in the fridge somehow. My boss didn't believe that for one second—but hey, the truth is stranger than fiction. Over time, I've learned to turn this into a kind of mutant superpower. When I lock in, I'm unstoppable—that's how I finished this book. The downside? My brain eventually taps out, and I have to eat a five-course meal and hibernate for a bit.

Spiritually, I sometimes lose sight of the bigger picture and greater purpose. I get so laser-focused on the immediate goal that I forget the "why" behind it. What helps me regain that perspective is my family and the legacy I want to leave. My ultimate goal—the heartbeat behind everything I do—is to be remembered as someone who came from nothing and built something meaningful in a foreign land. Someone who interacted with others with positivity and laughter, despite the challenges, and who never stopped striving to turn struggle into strength.

A problem is never just an obstacle—it's a moment that reveals how you think, what you fear, and how prepared you are to respond. How you define it determines whether you freeze, react, or move forward with intention.

Awareness & Clarity

"Knowing yourself is the beginning of all wisdom."
Aristotle

Awareness is the first step toward progress through recognizing your own patterns. It's the ability to notice your thoughts, feelings, and surroundings. It's seeing how your mindset, habits, and behaviors affect the outcome of every challenge. Without awareness, even the best strategies and tools fall apart.

Clarity, on the other hand, is the outcome of that awareness, resulting in a clear understanding of yourself, your goals, and the path to achieve them. You can't solve what you can't see. Clarity isn't always about knowing everything — it's about seeing things for what they truly are. In PRS clarity represents the ability to pause, observe, and define your situation before reacting to it. Most people make decisions out of confusion — they act on emotion, assumption, or fear. Clarity removes that fog for the next steps ahead.

When I talk about gaining awareness or building clarity, I'm really talking about the ability to identify three things:

1. Where you are — your current quadrant or mindset.
2. What's influencing you — your emotions, environment, or pressure points.
3. Where you need to go — your desired outcome or quadrant.

Once you know those three, every part of PRS — from the quadrant model to the 4A Framework — becomes easier to use. Clarity doesn't just help you see the road. It helps you drive it with purpose.

To me these two aspects shape every part of your being. Almost like wisdom, street smarts or common sense. Which we all know isn't quite common anymore. It enables us to ask ourselves questions: Do I know what I need to know? Is there something else I need to know more about? These questions open up your mind to think outside the box. It is that pioneer spirit for curiosity and learning?

The Band-Aid Problem

Most people don't fail because they can't solve problems. They fail because they keep solving the same problem over and over again. When something feels uncomfortable—stress, conflict, pressure, uncertainty— we instinctively try to make that feeling go away as fast as possible. We do something quick. We smooth it over. We push through. We distract ourselves. The discomfort fades, and we tell ourselves the problem is handled. But nothing actually changed.

That's what I mean by a band-aid solution. It doesn't actually fix the problem—it just quiets it. And quiet can feel like progress, even though it isn't. If you've ever wondered, why am I dealing with this again? This is usually why. The situation looks different, but the pattern is the same. The response worked just enough to get you through the moment, not enough to move you forward.

Awareness is recognizing when you're trying to feel better instead of see clearer.

Clarity is being honest about whether your actions changed the situation—or just reduced the tension. This is where PRS starts. Not with better answers, but with better observation. When you slow down long enough to notice what keeps repeating, you stop reacting on autopilot and start making intentional decisions instead.

Awareness doesn't solve problems by itself—but it creates the space where choice becomes possible. Without it, action is just reaction wearing a disguise.

Foundational Balance: The Three-Legged Stool

"You'll never regret investing in your health, learning, or relationships."

Unknown

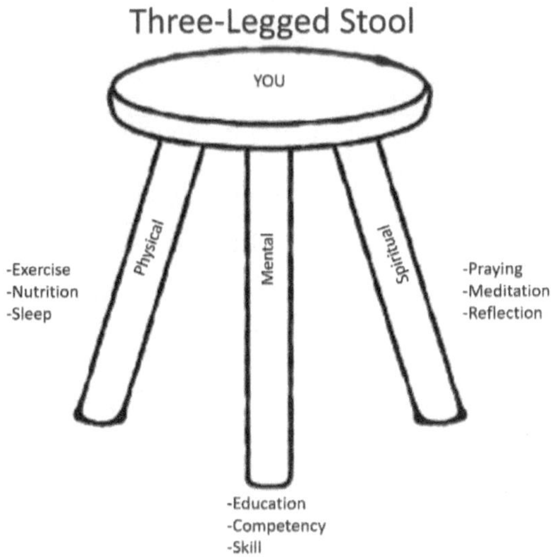

Illustration 8

Building a perfect balanced environment starts with oneself. Think of and picture a stool. It needs a minimum of three legs to stand and balance. If you take one away, it will not function and fall over. You can think of these three legs as the mind, body, and soul. **Mental, physical, & spiritual** wellbeing. Achieving balance among these three keeps someone better adapted to stress. Later in the book, I'll introduce my personal technique called the Three R's—Rest, Recover, Reset. A strategy I use whenever I find myself mentally, physically, or spiritually off balance. But for now, let's look at the three legs in more detail.

Physical

Physical fitness is not about appearance or performance—it's about capacity. It's hard, and often impossible, to show up consistently, think clearly, or make sound decisions when your body is constantly run down. If you are always sick, exhausted, or operating on empty, even the best intentions and systems will eventually fail.

Your physical state directly affects your mentality. Lack of sleep clouds judgment. Poor nutrition drains energy and patience. Chronic stress without movement tightens the body and narrows perspective. Over time, these conditions don't just impact health—they influence how you respond to problems. Fatigue increases reactivity. Discomfort shortens tolerance. Low energy amplifies frustration. What feels like a mindset issue is often a physical one.

PRS treats physical well-being as foundational, not optional. Exercise, balanced nutrition, and adequate sleep aren't self-care luxuries—they're functional requirements for sustained momentum.

You don't need extreme routines or perfect habits. You need consistency that supports clarity and resilience. Small, repeatable actions—daily movement, reasonable eating, intentional rest—compound into stability over time.

When your body is supported, your mentality becomes steadier. You're better able to pause instead of react, reflect instead of rush, and persist without burning out. Physical fitness doesn't solve your problems, but it raises your capacity to deal with them. In PRS, that capacity matters. Because progress isn't just about what you know or intend—it's about whether you have the energy to follow through.

Mental

Mental and emotional well-being are closely connected. How you think affects how you feel, and how you feel affects how you think. When one is off, the other usually follows. Together, they shape how you interpret situations, make decisions, and respond under pressure.

Mental strength is about clarity and preparedness. It's your ability to process information, think through situations, and make decisions without getting overwhelmed. Emotional strength is about regulation and awareness—recognizing what you're feeling without letting those emotions control your actions. When both are working together, you're able to pause, assess, and respond instead of reacting.

When mental and emotional health are strained, problems feel heavier than they actually are. Small issues turn into big ones. Decisions get delayed or avoided. You may feel anxious, frustrated, or stuck—not because you're incapable, but because your internal system is overloaded.

In those moments, it's easy to confuse emotion with reality and urgency with importance.

PRS treats mental and emotional fitness as functional requirements, not abstract self-care concepts. Real life demands thinking and feeling at the same time. Money stress, career pressure, relationships, health concerns, parenting—none of these are purely logical or purely emotional. They require understanding *and* regulation.

Learning plays a key role here. When you don't understand a situation, uncertainty grows. And when uncertainty grows, emotions tend to fill the gap. That's why learning how money works can reduce anxiety, why gaining new skills can restore confidence, and why understanding your options can calm fear. Knowledge creates clarity, and clarity stabilizes emotion.

At the same time, emotional awareness matters just as much. Ignoring emotions doesn't make them disappear—it just lets them operate in the background. When emotions go unrecognized, they show up as impatience, avoidance, overreaction, or burnout. PRS doesn't ask you to suppress emotion; it teaches you to notice it, account for it, and respond with intention.

When mental clarity and emotional regulation work together, you gain control over how you move through problems. You're better able to slow down, separate signal from noise, and choose the right response. You don't need to have everything figured out—you just need enough awareness to move forward without panic or self-sabotage.

In PRS, mental and emotional well-being support balance. They help you stay steady when things are uncertain, flexible when plans change, and grounded when pressure builds. Problems don't disappear, but they stop running the show. And that's when real progress becomes possible.

Spiritual

Spiritual well-being means different things to different people. For me, it's about believing in something bigger than just myself—something that gives life meaning, direction, and purpose beyond day-to-day survival. Without that, life can start to feel mechanical: wake up, work, pay bills, get older, and repeat. That kind of existence might keep you busy, but it doesn't necessarily keep you grounded or fulfilled.

Spirituality doesn't have to be religious. Religion can be part of it, but it doesn't have to be. Some people find meaning through faith. Others through nature, the universe, service, legacy, or connection to humanity. What matters is the belief that your life and actions are part of something larger—that what you do carries weight beyond the moment you're in.

When you believe in something bigger, your decisions change. You start thinking beyond short-term gain and immediate relief. For example, someone under financial pressure who believes life is only about survival might justify harmful choices just to get by. But when you believe your actions matter—to others, to the future, to something greater—you naturally draw boundaries around what you're willing to do. Purpose creates restraint. Meaning shapes behavior.

PRS treats spiritual well-being as the moral and directional anchor of the system. It's what keeps problem-solving from becoming reckless or purely self-serving. It reminds you that how you move forward matters just as much as moving forward itself.

Practices like prayer, meditation, reflection, or time in nature can strengthen this connection. They slow you down, create perspective, and reconnect you to what matters most. You don't need to have all the answers—you just need a sense that your life has meaning and that your actions contribute to something beyond immediate outcomes.

When spiritual grounding is present, problems don't feel pointless. Challenges feel like refinement instead of punishment. Change feels like part of a larger process instead of chaos. In PRS, spiritual well-being supports balance by keeping you aligned with your values, your purpose, and the kind of person you want to be—especially when pressure is high.

Balance isn't something you achieve once—it's something you constantly adjust. When one leg weakens, awareness lets you compensate before everything tips over.

The Power of Mindset and Mentality

"The problem is not the problem; it's your attitude about the problem."
Ann Brashares

I recently watched a short video showing the importance of mindset and attitude. It stated that there was a difference between having an optimistic, positive, growth-oriented mindset versus a pessimistic, negative, and defeatist mindset. This correlated down to the cellular level because our bodies generate a frequency, or synergy, based on our emotions and mindset. Negative emotions like anger, fear, and blame feed off each other and set the tone for the rest of our attitude. In short, your mindset fuels your joy or your misery. Let's look at this in motion. If you wake up late for work and as you rush in someone cuts you off in traffic, this will set the stage for the rest of your day. You finally get to work and tell everyone about your experience and how angry you are. This causes you unknowingly and subconsciously to overlook the positive facets of the day such as your coworker who just got promoted or even getting a compliment on your work. Instead, you might even feel jealous of your coworker's promotion or think your boss just said 'good job' because they knew you were having a bad day.

It's best to deal with emotions and experiences and move on. In these moments, I like to play the what-if game. Instead of spiraling, I pause and reframe the events of the day. Consider our example: What if your body and mind were so tired that they needed the extra hour of sleep? What if the guy who cut you off has a dying family member in the hospital, and this might be the last time they can see them? None of this may be true. But that's not the point. The point is, your mindset is a choice. And that choice shapes your emotional state, you attitude, and how you show up for the rest of the day. You can either stay stuck in negativity or you can create flow by shifting how you interpret the moment. When you reframe it like this, try to release tension, reclaim presence, and make better decisions. Sometimes I use the delay to call a friend, catch up on an audiobook, or just enjoy some peace in the chaos. That's what I call turning bad stress into good stress. That stress that sharpens you, not shatters you. What ideas can you think of to try in that pause moment?

Ultimately, the key is knowing we can't control everything and sometimes we just need to go with the flow. Your attitude doesn't just react to problems. It ends up creating the conditions for how you experience them. Whether you're stuck in a quadrant of fear, impulsiveness, overthinking, or achievement, your mindset determines whether you spin or shift. You can't always control the external chaos, but you can influence how you move through it. Illustration shows that the same mindset and habits end up with the same results. However, a new mindset and new habits lead to new results. It may not be the best results, but at least it is different, and you can build from there. Change it up a bit. Experiment. This is the PRS at its very core. You cannot have a new reality with an old mentality.

Problem Re-Solving System Activity

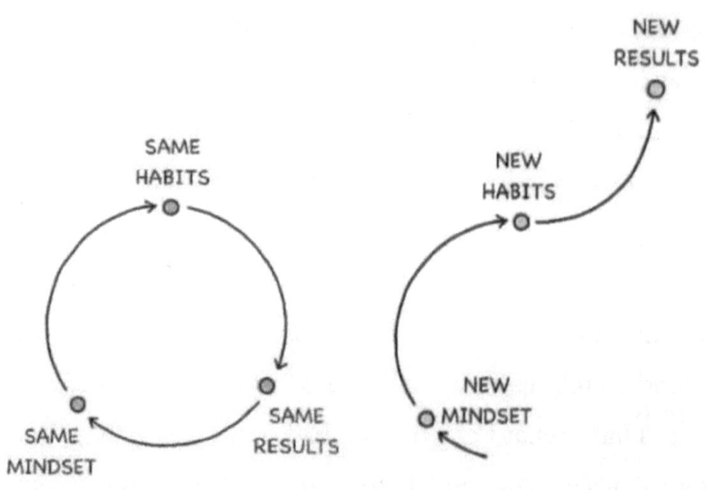

Illustration 9

During one of my deployments, I met Joseph, a septic truck driver. Despite the heat, low pay, and horrible conditions, Joseph was always smiling. My duties were to escort him as he drove around and pump out the latrines. At the end of the day, he was covered in feces and smelled horrible. Yet this guy was the definition of a happy optimist. If glass half full were a person, it would totally be him. I believe he said he made what equaled to $20 a day. It was still a lot for his home country of India, and he sent it all home in a process called repatriation.

I'll never forget the day we had to clear an overfilled septic tank. When he started pumping into the truck, the hose got stuck somehow, and I had to go over and help maneuver this thing around. We managed to get it loose, but it was overfilling, and it popped out like some giant sandworm from Dune. It was erupting and spewing poop everywhere. I immediately got sick and felt like I lost every meal I'd eaten in my lifetime. Joseph just laughed it off and kept working. His attitude has stuck with me along with his work ethic, optimism, and perspective. I often wonder what he is doing now.

Common Mindset Towards Problems

"Running away from any problem only increases
the distance from the solution."
Unknown

We all have faced, or will eventually face some type of problem, challenge, or change in our lives. These obstacles come in many forms: personal setbacks, career roadblocks, financial struggles, health crises, or unexpected life changes. While the nature of the problem may differ from person to person, one universal truth remains: Our responses determine our outcome.

Everyone reacts and responds differently to stimuli. Some people tackle issues head-on, while others retreat, overthink, or avoid dealing with them altogether. But the consensus is that most people instinctively think and react negatively to problems. Instead of seeing challenges as opportunities for growth, they often feel like they are more of burdens, threats, or roadblocks.

One of the biggest reasons for this negative reaction is fear. I tell my kids my definition of fear is **False Events Appearing Real**. Our fears are often based on imagined threats or exaggerated consequences rather than actual evidence, leading to anxiety, hesitation, and inaction.

There are many faces of fear including fear of failure, the unknown, judgment, change, and of making the wrong decision. When we let these fears dominate our thinking, they become a fog that clouds our judgment and stalls our progress. But fear doesn't just block our path. It convinces us there's no path at all.

Unchecked fear causes people to freeze in their tracks, to be stuck in a mental loop that prevents progress. We delay, we avoid, we procrastinate. And the longer we stay in that state, the harder it is to climb out. The problem doesn't go away. It grows, feeding on our silence and inaction. This reminds me of those cartoons where someone sees a ghost. Immediately, they freeze solid and cannot move or even run away, even though their life depends on it. Below are some reasons why we freeze when faced with problems, even when it makes us miserable:

- **Being Overwhelmed** – The sheer size or complexity of a problem can feel paralyzing. When there are too many moving parts or consequences to consider, we get stuck trying to make sense of it all instead of taking one simple first step.

- **Fear of Failure** – Many people hesitate to act because they worry about making mistakes or looking foolish. The truth is, failure isn't the opposite of success—it's part of it. But fear twists that reality and makes inaction seem safer.

- **Lack of Control** – When a situation feels outside our influence, it's easy to slip into helplessness. We say things like, "It's out of my hands," or "What's the point?" even though there are usually still things within our power to change.

- **Analysis Paralysis** – Overthinking every possible outcome can be just as dangerous as acting without thinking at all. We spend so much time playing mental chess that we never move a single piece.

- **Past Experiences** – If someone has tried and failed before, that emotional scar can cast a shadow on every new attempt. They carry the weight of old failures into new challenges and assume history will repeat itself.

Unfortunately, inaction becomes a coping mechanism that adds to the burden. The problem seems even more insurmountable the longer we wait to face it. So how do we break free? It starts with awareness. Recognize fear for what it is: a natural reaction, not a life sentence. Once we name the fear, we can shrink its power. The next crucial step is taking action, no matter how small. A single decision, a single step forward, can cut through the fog. Action builds confidence. Confidence weakens fear. Momentum builds with every move we make.

They say more people are afraid of public speaking than of death. I could not agree more. When I took a public speaking class in college, we had various assignments that including presenting informative, demonstrative, and persuasive speeches. I found it quite easy to write about the things I knew and cared about. For my demonstration, I brought a mini-kitchen with me to class along with my mother. She assisted me, showing how to make lumpias, bite-sized egg rolls you cannot just eat one of. They are the first dish to go to parties. We rolled a couple, deep-fried them, and passed them around class. That was the only A that I got that semester. The lesson here is that while my fear of public speaking was there and quite real, I didn't let fear freeze me. I chose a topic that I knew intimately and cared deeply about. I not only overcame my fear; I actually excelled at the task. If we are concerned about our problems and find the value in solving, then fears become a minor nuisance.

Fear doesn't disappear when you notice it—but it loses control when you recognize it. What matters isn't whether fear shows up, but whether it gets to decide your next move.

From Fixed to Fluid: Change Your Perspective

"What we think determines what happens to us, so if we want to change our lives, we need to stretch our minds.
Unknown

When tackling any problem, challenge, or change—whether health-related, financial, relational, simple, or complex—having the right approach is key. Instead of seeing problems as immovable obstacles, what if we treated them as puzzles to be solved with every challenge being an opportunity to learn, grow, and develop new strategies? This small mindset shift, focusing on solutions instead of barriers, can drastically change how we approach life's inevitable difficulties.

Think about this. The most successful people aren't the ones who have never faced problems. They're the ones who learn how to work through them. They train themselves to move past fear and hesitation, taking action even in uncertainty. Instead of freezing when faced with a challenge, ask yourself:

- What is one small step I can take right now?
- What can I control in this situation?
- Who can I reach out to for guidance or support?

By developing a proactive mindset, we turn problems from paralyzing fears into manageable tasks and that's the first step toward resolution. A phrase I picked up in the military sums this up well: **adapt, overcome,** and **improvise.** This mindset reflects the ability to stay flexible in uncertain situations, find solutions where none seem to exist, and push forward despite adversity. Life is unpredictable, and not everything will go according to plan. Those who can adjust their approach on the fly are often the ones who emerge stronger. Learning to reframe obstacles as opportunities allows you to take setbacks in stride and turn them into stepping stones for growth. Here is how to apply this mindset:

- **Adapt** – Be willing to change your approach and shift strategies when needed. The ability to pivot in response to new information is key.

- **Overcome** – Develop fortitude to push past obstacles rather than letting them define you.
- **Improvise** – Think outside the box. Use creativity, and make use of the resources available to you.

Imagine someone dealing with unexpected financial stress. A fixed perspective sounds like this: I'm stuck. I don't make enough money. There's nothing I can do right now. That mindset freezes action and narrows options. The problem feels permanent, heavy, and personal.

A fluid perspective sounds different: This is a problem to work through, not a dead end. Instead of panicking, the focus shifts to movement. What expenses can be reduced this month? What skills could be improved to increase income? Who can offer advice or perspective? The situation hasn't magically disappeared—but the response has changed. Clarity replaces overwhelm. Small steps replace paralysis.

The same applies to health challenges, career setbacks, or relationship strain. A fixed mindset asks, why is this happening to me? A fluid mindset asks, What's the next right move? That shift doesn't guarantee easy outcomes, but it restores control—and control is where momentum begins.

In PRS, this shift is essential. Fluid thinking allows you to adapt when plans change, overcome obstacles without losing yourself, and improvise when conditions aren't ideal. You stop waiting for certainty and start moving with intention. You don't need to solve everything at once—you just need to stay in motion.

Moving from fixed to fluid isn't about being positive or pretending things are easy. It's about staying flexible instead of getting stuck. When you do that, problems become clearer, challenges feel manageable, and change stops knocking you off balance. Whether it's managing finances, navigating markets, or making decisions in fast-changing environments, progress often depends on the ability to adapt, overcome, and improvise rather than freeze when conditions shift.

There's a difference between preparing for a situation and entering it with the right mentality. How you think going in matters more than most people realize. We've all had these thoughts before: I think it'll work out. I hope it works out. I know it'll work out. Those statements sound similar, but they don't carry the same weight. Confidence that's grounded in preparation changes how you act, how long you persist, and how you respond when things don't go as planned.

A fluid mindset doesn't mean uncertainty disappears—it means you stop letting uncertainty stall you. Flexibility is what allows progress to continue when conditions change.

Personal Example: Trusting the Process

"What we think determines what happens to us, so if we want to change our lives, we need to stretch our minds."
Unknown

I was reminded of this during a stressful period when my family needed to move in the middle of an unpredictable housing market. We did everything right on paper—planning, searching, adjusting expectations—yet deal after deal fell apart. Homes we wanted went under contract quickly. One even came back on the market, only to fall through again. At the same time, we were trying to coordinate selling our own home. It felt like every step forward came with a setback.

There were moments when it would have been easy to force a decision out of frustration or panic—settling for something that didn't fit just to be done with the process. Instead, we stayed patient, kept preparing, and trusted the timing rather than reacting to pressure. Eventually, the right opportunity reopened at the right moment. The conditions finally aligned in a way that allowed both sides to move forward without forcing the outcome. Looking back, it wasn't luck—it was mentality. Persistence without panic. Preparation without desperation. Trust without passivity.

This is what PRS teaches when it comes to mentality. You don't control timing, markets, or outcomes—but you do control how you show up. When your mindset is steady, setbacks don't knock you off course. They inform your next move. When you stop trying to force results, things tend to make more sense. Sometimes progress isn't about pushing harder—it's about staying ready long enough for the right moment to arrive.

You Are the Variable: Taking Ownership of Your Life

"If you don't like the road you're walking, start paving another one."
Unknown

Accountability is the bridge between awareness and action, turns intention into action, and transforms challenges into opportunities for growth. It's the willingness to take responsibility for your choices, your effort, and your results—without excuses or blame. When you hold yourself accountable, you stop waiting for someone else to fix your situation and start owning the direction of your life. In problem re-solving, accountability is the foundation of progress. You can't change what you don't claim. It demands honesty, consistency, and courage—the kind that says this is my life, and I'm responsible for where it goes from here.

One of the most empowering lessons in life is this: You are not a passenger; you are the driver and. e in control of your life. If you are not enjoying where you are going, simply change it. The moment you realize that you're not stuck, you're not trapped, and that you always can change your situation, everything shifts. Problems, challenges, and changes are inevitable, but we have control over how we respond to them. Taking ownership means acknowledging that we have the power to adapt, shift, and overcome rather than letting obstacles define us.

I often remind myself and my kids of a quote that became a personal mantra: "If you didn't change something in your life, you chose it." That may sound harsh at first, but it's also incredibly freeing. It means that we're not powerless. We may not control every event that happens to us, but we absolutely control how we respond to them.

Taking ownership isn't about blaming yourself for everything that goes wrong. It's about recognizing that your future isn't dictated by your past. That's your decision. Even the small ones. Stack up and create the life you're living. If you're unhappy with that life, then change starts with you.

Life will always hand us problems, challenges, and change. That's a guarantee. Just like death and taxes. But ownership means we stop pointing fingers and start making moves. We stop waiting for permission and start taking action. Ownership transforms people from victims of circumstance into creators of opportunity. It starts small:

- Choose to speak up instead of staying silent.
- Apply for that new position even if you're unsure.
- Say no when something doesn't align with your values.
- Invest time into your growth even when you're tired.

And it grows into something powerful: the belief that you can steer your life in a better direction. If something goes wrong at a company, say a cyber security attack, things cannot be fixed without first taking accountability. Sure, maybe some heads will roll. Maybe even yours if this was your responsibility, but at the end of the day not, taking ownership of what happened will only stall re-solving matters.

Ownership isn't about fault—it's about control. The moment you accept that you're the variable, you regain the ability to change direction instead of waiting for circumstances to do it for you.

The Power of Reflection

"Don't dwell on what went wrong. Instead, focus on what to do next. Spend your energies on moving forward toward finding the answer."
Denis Waitley

Reflection, for me, is a mindset and a routine that's an essential foundation for success. I practice prayer, meditation, or reflection. They all serve the same function helpings with stress reduction, clarity in decision making and strengthening inner resolve. For me prayer gives me hope in tough times and good times. Meditation provides peace, tranquility, and mental rest during the day. Reflection offers clarity and focuses on what I did great, where can I help, how can I grow.

This is important because life is a continuous cycle of ups and downs. One day you will be on top and the next be on the bottom. From my experience, the key to surviving the cycle is balance. In a manner of speaking, force the cycle of up by going down a bit and force the cycle of down by going up a bit. can create affirmation for focus or journal for reflection, meditation, or clarity. It all clears your mind and prepares you for the times ahead. Prayer, or reflection, helps align one's thoughts before taking action, making it a powerful tool for the PRS.

In tough times, I lean more so on prayer to be hopeful and find strength to keep going, knowing things will not always be this way. Just have to maintain resilience like a firm-rooted palm tree during a hurricane. It also makes me grateful for the things I already have or have accomplished thus far. Most people measure success only by financial or social standings. They cannot see other successes such as health, family, or relationships. You might not be rich in financial terms, but you may be rich in family or relationships. Things can always be worse than your current situation. You could be living in a cramped apartment with so many people but at least you have an apartment. Millions of people would trade with you. At the same time this gives you resolve and something to work for. That American dream of owning a home with a yard, that opens up a whole can of worms that we will not get into here. Focus on finding the good things in life.

In good times, use prayer to stay humble and maintain perspective, knowing once again that things will not always be this way. Be even more grateful for the circumstances, opportunities, and relationships you have. For example, maybe you are gainfully employed, even if you don't get paid your dream salary, but you are just grateful to be working as other people cannot even work because of other hardships like health, the job market, etc.

I pray, meditate, and reflect about myself twice a day: when I wake up and before I go to bed. In the morning, I reflect on how grateful I am to get another day. For all my gamers out there, it is like loading a save file. Another day to continue the journey. Fix the wrongs or right mistakes from the previous day. If I had any dreams that night, I try to write them down to analyze later. They say that dreams are windows into the subconscious mind revealing our innermost wants and fears. For those that journal, this is the opportune time to plan out your day and reflect on things that were not accomplished the day before due to time constraints, set up priorities, positive affirmations, among other things.

Before I go to sleep every night, I reflect on what I accomplished that day today, measuring it against the day before, noting any progress and frustrations. I ask myself, am I a better person today than yesterday? Did I learn something new, practice something I am not good at, help someone, etc. The answer should always be yes. I pray for peace, a good night's sleep, and to start the next day refreshed.

An elderly man I met at the gas station on my way to work inspired me to start this routine. While waiting in line for my coffee and bagel, I said hello and asked him how he was doing. He said he was just grateful to wake up today and be able to live another day to the fullest, whether it's good or bad. Just being alive is good enough. That got me thinking. Here I am dreading waking up, getting dressed, going to work, being in traffic, and just not grateful for another day given to me. This complete stranger will never know how thankful I am thankful for this life lesson that I will use for the rest of my life.

Using this mindset, combined with the wisdom from a friend of mine from my military days, I created an exercise for my pillars of meaning, and look for ways to improve my life based on them. Taking care of your pillars enables you to be the best version of yourself and your community.

- **Social & Professional pillar**: Catch up with family and friends.
- **Spiritual Pillar:** Dedicate a few minutes each day for prayer, reading scriptures, journaling, gratitude, meditating, doing yoga, or other thing you find spiritual.
- **Mental Pillar:** Read, and practice mindfulness.
- **Physical Pillar:** Eat whole foods, walk or exercise, create a balanced sleeping routine.
- **Financial Pillar:** Live within your means and plan for your financial future.

Reflection turns experience into instruction. Without it, life keeps repeating the same lessons—louder each time.

Resilience & Persistence the Inner Power Source: Determination, Dedication, Discipline

"Your dreams don't stop; you do."

Victor Gilmore

Resilience & Triad of Success

	DETERMINATION	DEDICATION	DISCIPLINE
Primary Focus	The firm resolve to achieve a difficult goal despite obstacles.	An emotional and loyal commitment to a goal or a cause.	The controlled, consistent action required to achieve a goal, even when you don't feel like it.
Core Driver	Inner drive and grit; the motivation to not give up.	Passion and emotional investment in the outcome.	Rules and habits; a consistent set of actions.
Role in the process	**The initiation**. It is the initial decision and the inner strength that pushes you to begin and keep trying after setbacks.	**The commitment**. It keeps the passion alive for the long haul, especially when the day-to-day work becomes a grind.	**The action**. It is the daily practice of doing the work and avoiding distractions. It is the bridge between dreams and reality.
The Why vs How	Addresses the "**why**"—the reason you keep going.	Addresses the "**why**"—the passion and emotional investment that makes the goal important.	Addresses the "**how**"—the day-to-day actions and routines required to make progress.
Analogy	**The compass**: The compass is set on a destination and provides the firm resolve to stay the course.	**The fuel**: The fuel powers the engine, providing the energy to keep the journey moving.	**The steering wheel**: The steering wheel controls the daily decisions and specific actions needed to navigate the path.

Illustration 10

I talk a lot in this book about mindset, ownership, and reflection. But there's a deeper secret that anchors long-term transformation. I call it the resilience and persistence. Nathan McCurry from Medium lists the three Ds of Success: **determination**, **dedication** and **discipline**. Think of these as the fuel for your power source. These three aren't flashy. They don't come easily. But they're often the difference between repeating cycles and rewriting your story. When these three traits work together, you don't just survive. You rebuild. You rise. You reinvent yourself.

Resilience and **persistence** get a lot of praise. But most people treat them like personality traits. Something you either have or don't. But from what I've seen in my life, and in the lives of other people I deeply respect, they are built, not innate. They're the result of something deeper; something developed I want to share Victor's story. We met at a community event focused on nonviolence. I was there to support the mission. I didn't expect to walk away with a reminder of everything this chapter stands for.

Victor grew up in a household shaped by dysfunction, addiction, and abuse. His father, an alcoholic, passed away from liver disease when Victor was around 10 years old. With no father figure, limited support, and early exposure to trauma, Victor leaned into football as an outlet. He played little league, tasting victory with a winning team. But like many kids left on the sidelines emotionally, things started to slide downward.

As he got older, loneliness kicked in. So did the weed, alcohol, and bad influences. In his teenage years, Victor's life shifted into survival mode. He stole, robbed, and did whatever he could to survive and suppress the chaos inside. His first prison sentence came at just 18 years old. Over time, Victor served three major sentences, the last one was for over 16 years. But that's not the story I want to end with, because that's not the man I met.

In prison, Victor found something rare. A spark of ownership. He started journaling, planning, and taking classes. Learning barbering allowed him independence, even behind bars. More importantly, he built a vision. One that included not just a skill set, but a lifestyle such as working in mobile barbering and mobile detailing He also earned a Commercial Driver's License (CDL). Now he is building a marriage and finally living out a plan he wrote years earlier.

When he cut my hair at that event, he wasn't just offering a service. He was living proof that resilience, determination, dedication, and discipline are transformational. Even when you start from rock bottom. Now, let's break down resilience, persistence, and determination. .

Resilience

Resilience is the ability to bounce back from setbacks and adversity. In pursuing your goals, you'll inevitably face challenges, obstacles, and failures. It's your resilience that will determine whether you get back on track or give up.

Victor lost his father, his stability, and eventually his freedom, but he didn't lose his ability to get back up. Life knocked him down over and over, but he never stayed down. Resilience doesn't mean you don't suffer. It means you choose to rise again. This time smarter, stronger, and more grounded.

Persistence

Persistence is the will to keep moving forward no matter how long the road becomes. It's the quiet, stubborn drive that refuses to quit even when progress feels invisible. Where resilience helps you recover, persistence helps you continue.

Victor didn't rebuild his life overnight—he stayed consistent, doing the small things every day that moved him closer to freedom, stability, and peace. Persistence is showing up when it's inconvenient, pushing through fatigue, and believing that small steps still count when the finish line feels far away. It's the heartbeat that keeps you advancing when motivation fades and only discipline remains.

Determination

Determination means a strong decision or intention to achieve something, even when faced with difficulties, and the quality of continuing to try achieve something despite obstacles.

After multiple setbacks. Including a return to prison. Victor didn't quit. He wrote goals and made plans. Even when nothing around him supported those dreams, he kept moving forward. That's determination. It's not energy. Something deeper than motivation fueled his drive to come out on top.

Dedication

Dedication is strong, wholehearted commitment and devotion to a person, purpose, or task, often involving consistent effort, loyalty, and perseverance to achieve a goal or uphold an ideal. It requires placing a priority on that commitment, which can manifest as sacrificing personal desires for the sake of a cause, showing unwavering support, or consistently putting in work and time.

Victor didn't just want to change; he committed to it. He had every reason to give up, but something in him stated that this life I see in my mind is worth fighting for. That vision kept him focused. Dedication isn't passive. It's what fuels your why when life keeps punching and kicking you in the face.

Discipline

Discipline is the training and practice of self-control, order, and obedience to rules, often to achieve goals or improve one's character. It encompasses the ability to regulate one's actions, emotions, and thoughts, even when facing temptation or difficulty. Discipline might mean leaving our desires on the sidelines and embracing what is necessary instead.

Prison is a place where many lose themselves. But Victor used it as a crucible for transformation. He learned a trade, took classes, and refined a future he hadn't yet stepped into. Now, he lives out that plan every day. Barbering. Driving. Showing up. Serving others. That's discipline, not sexy, not instant, but real.

Victor's life isn't perfect. Neither is mine. Neither is yours. But stories like his prove that change is possible when the inner foundation is strong. If you're feeling stuck, look inward. Determination, dedication and discipline won't just get you through a problem They'll give you the structure to build a new future. When we build our inner engine with a refusal to quit, we gain an infinite ability to rebuild ourselves and transform our lives.

Resilience and persistence without direction leads to exhaustion. Resilience with clarity builds momentum. The difference is knowing why you're pushing—and when to pause.

Creating Balance and Maintain Momentum

"Balance is not something you find; it's something you create."

Unknown

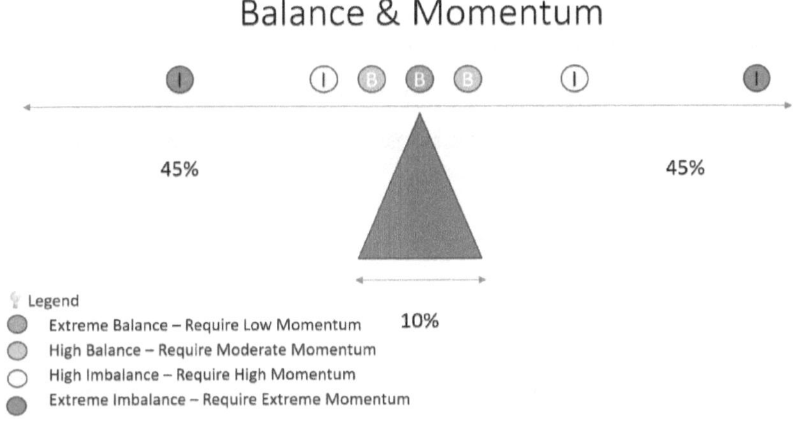

Illustration 11

One of the most critical aspects of PRS is finding balance between action and reflection, effort and recovery, persistence and adaptability. Without balance, we either burn out from excessive action or remain stuck in hesitation and fear. Many people get caught in extremes either rushing into solutions without thinking or over analyzing every decision without taking action.

Balance is not about avoiding problems. It's about approaching them with the right energy, mindset, and rhythm to keep progressing. The goal is finding the middle ground where preparation, execution, and adaptation work together harmoniously. Perfect balance is optimal, but 90% is still acceptable and preferred. The amount of effort required to achieve one or two percent gains is not worth it. Once balance is established, momentum is necessary to sustain progress and prevent regression. As one loses balance, more and more momentum is required to regain balance.

Momentum builds when small, consistent actions compound over time. Instead of focusing on massive changes all at once, a more effective approach is to create repeatable habits that generate small wins and maintain motivation. Avoiding extended breaks in progress is key. Missing one day might be recoverable, but two in a row can derail momentum.

Rather than measuring progress solely by the outcome, tracking small milestones and improvements along the way ensures motivation remains high. Momentum doesn't always mean pushing forward at full speed; sometimes strategic pacing helps you avoid burnout. Recognizing when to slow down, reassess, or adjust course is just as important as staying consistent.

Another factor that influences momentum is your environment and support systems. Surrounding yourself with people, information, and environments that encourage growth fuels ongoing success. Whether through like-minded individuals, educational content, or structured systems, having the right influences can reinforce discipline and accountability.

Finding balance ensures you don't fall into extremes, while building momentum ensures you don't stay stuck. By integrating these principles into your daily actions, you not only resolve problems but you develop a system for sustained success.

I battle through this effort of balance and momentum with my finances which seem to hang by a thread. Because of the size of my family, a wrong move, an unexpected bill, a delayed payment, or a medical emergency can tip everything over. That's where the real test of balance begins. Some months require slowing down and reassessing priorities, while others demand quick action to stay ahead. I've learned that financial balance isn't about having endless income; it's about maintaining awareness, control, and discipline even when resources feel stretched thin. Momentum, on the other hand, is the small, consistent progress — tracking expenses, cutting unnecessary costs, building an emergency fund — that turns anxiety into stability. It's not about perfection; it's about direction. Each intentional step, no matter how small, keeps the wheel of progress turning, and that's what ultimately restores peace in both finances and mindset.

Mentality determines how you show up before you ever act. It shapes your interpretation of problems, your tolerance for discomfort, and your willingness to adapt. In the next chapter, we'll move from mindset to behavior—looking at how these internal patterns show up in real actions, habits, and responses. Awareness sets the stage. What you do with it determines the outcome.

Strengthen Your Mentality

"You can't have a new reality with an old mentality."

Let this remind you that every meaningful transformation starts with a mental upgrade. When you're thinking evolves, your reality follows. Your journey depends on how you think, especially under pressure. A strong mindset doesn't appear overnight—it's forged through repetition, reflection, and small, consistent acts of self-discipline. Use these quick steps to reinforce what you've learned in this chapter and begin putting the strategy of mindset and attitude into motion. This practice is designed to take 10–15 minutes total. Don't overthink your answers. The goal is awareness, not perfection. Write your answers in a notebook or phone note app. Over time, you'll start to see patterns—the real "diagnostics" of your internal battery.

Step 1 – Daily Check-In. At the start or end of each day, ask yourself:

- What emotion is steering my attitude today—fear, frustration, or focus?

- Did I let outside events control my energy, or did I choose my response?

- Did I try to make a problem feel better today—or understand it better?

- One word that defines how I want to *show up* tomorrow is:

____.

Step 2 – Fuel Adjustments. Mentality is your fuel. Micro-refuels prevent burnout and keep your internal engine running clean. When your energy runs low, try one of the following:

1. **Refill:** Take five slow breaths, stretch, or step outside for one minute of silence.

2. **Refocus:** Say out loud one truth about yourself that grounds you (e.g., *"I've handled worse before."*)

3. **Recharge:** Do one action that aligns with your mission—however small.

Step 3 – Reframe Your Thought Loop. Do this once per day for a week when negative self-talk appears; you'll start retraining your automatic responses.

1. **Catch it:** Write the thought exactly as it showed up.

2. **Challenge it:** Ask, "Is this fact or fear?"

3. **Change it:** Replace it with a constructive belief that still feels honest. *(Example: "I'm behind"* → *"I'm learning at my pace, and progress is progress.")*

Step 4 – Momentum Micro-Win. Pick one 5-minute action that supports the mentality you're building. This is not about habit perfection—it's about reinforcing movement. Aim to return to this action most days over the next week. If you miss a day, don't reset or quit—simply resume the next time you remember. Momentum is built by returning, not by being flawless. Only add or change the habit once it feels supportive, not forced. Missing a day doesn't break momentum—quitting does.

Examples include:

- Journaling
- Stretching
- Reading a paragraph from this book
- Pausing to plan one small next step

Step 5 – Reflect & Reset. At the end of the week, review your notes and circle any words or phrases that repeat. These patterns reveal your dominant mentality.

Ask yourself: *Does this mentality fuel me or drain me?*

If it drains you, adjust—not by pushing harder, but by choosing a more intentional thought, action, or boundary for the next week. PRS isn't about discipline through pressure. It's about alignment through awareness.

KEY INSIGHTS FOR CHAPTER 4

- **Problems, challenges, and change are unavoidable—but they are not the same.** Problems require solutions, challenges test resilience, and change demands adaptability. Recognizing the difference determines how you respond instead of react.

- **Awareness and clarity are always the first step.** Before action comes understanding. Awareness acts as a navigational tool, helping you choose intentional responses rather than default reactions when facing problems, challenges, or change.

- **The Three-Legged Stool creates balance.** Mental, physical, and spiritual well-being must be maintained together. Ignoring any one leg creates instability that shows up as burnout, poor decisions, or stalled progress.

- **FEAR (False Events Appearing Real) is one of the biggest barriers to action.** Fear of failure, uncertainty, or past experiences can freeze momentum. Progress resumes when fear is challenged, reframed, and broken down into small, controllable steps.

- **Mindset determines how you move forward.** Fixed thinking leads to avoidance, overthinking, or impulsive reactions. A fluid mindset—adapt, overcome, and improvise—keeps you flexible, responsive, and solution-oriented under pressure.

- **Mentality is your internal power source.** Your thoughts, emotions, and self-talk directly influence your energy and outcomes. Reframing negative thought loops restores control and turns stress into forward momentum.

- **Small, intentional actions build momentum.** You don't need perfect habits to make progress. Consistent micro-wins—done most days and resumed when missed—create sustainable movement without pressure or burnout.

- **Ownership restores agency.** If nothing changes, you've chosen acceptance. Taking responsibility for how you think, respond, and act is the starting point for meaningful and lasting improvement.

- **Reflection sustains balance.** Prayer, meditation, or quiet reflection help you reset perspective, recognize patterns, and realign your mentality—especially during difficult or uncertain seasons.

- **Resilience and persistence are built, not born.** They grow through consistent determination, dedication, and discipline—the Triad of Success. Applied daily, they don't just help you recover; they help you move forward stronger.

- **Balance and momentum work together.** Balance prevents burnout; momentum creates progress. When both are present, small steps compound into clarity, stability, and long-term growth.

Behavior & Actions

"Don't waste your time trying to control the uncontrollable, or trying to solve the unsolvable, or think about what could have been."
David Mahoney

There comes a point in every challenge where we must decide—act now, pause and think, or step back entirely. You've likely felt each of those impulses before hesitation comes from fear. Reckless bursts of action that come from frustration. Thoughtful pauses turn into endless analysis. These aren't random moods; they're behavioral patterns that quietly dictate how we handle problems, challenges, and change.

Most people don't actually struggle with having problems—they struggle with knowing what to do about them. Should I wait? Should I move? Do I need more information? Should I just push through? When we reach that internal crossroads, the question isn't just what's wrong, but how we can respond to what's wrong.

This is where the PRS quadrant model comes in. It gives you a lens through which to understand your patterns before taking action.

Think of it as a mirror and a map. The mirror reveals your natural tendencies, and the map shows your potential routes forward. This model doesn't label you—it equips you. By identifying your current approach, you gain clarity, emotional control, and the ability to make sustainable progress instead of repeating cycles of reaction and regret. Think back to our analogy of the system and car components. This is your steering wheel to navigate the roads of life.

The quadrant model is built around two intersecting forces: actions and reflection. Every decision sits somewhere on this grid. On one axis lies low to high action—how much initiative or energy you bring. On the other lies low to high reflection—how deeply you think before moving. Where these two meet determines your current quadrant and, ultimately, your behavior.

Imagine these quadrants as rooms in a house you can walk through. In one corner is hesitation and fear; in another, overthinking; in another, impulsive motion; and in the center, balance. The goal isn't to stay locked in one room—it's learning how to move freely between them.

I created the quadrant model because I needed to make sense of my behavior. There were times when I charged into problems too fast without a plan, and times when I over thought everything and got stuck doing nothing. Sometimes I hesitated out of fear, and sometimes I acted on impulse. And what I realized is that how we approach problems matters just as much as the tools we used to fix them.

This model is flexible. You'll discover that different problems may place you in different quadrants, and that's okay. For example, you might be decisive at work but fearful in your relationships, or you might be an overthinker in your career but impulsive in financial decisions. The point isn't perfection; it's awareness. So, before you take your next step, let's figure out where you're starting from. This is your steering wheel to get from stuck to unstoppable.

I've seen all four personas in action, not just in others, but in myself in high-stress deployments, family arguments, business decisions, and sleepless nights full of uncertainty. I've moved between these quadrants more times than I can count. That's why this chapter matters. When you know who you are at the moment, you can plan your next move better.

This chapter breaks down those quadrants and the personas that define them. We'll go beyond just naming them. You'll learn what motivates each persona, what holds them back, and what type of problems they're best suited for. You'll also recognize your own tendencies and where you land most often, because identifying your default quadrant is the first step to growth. Here is what we will cover:

- Model which is your behavior and actions — it shows how you're handling the road ahead, how you behave under stress, and when you're drifting off course.
- The sections and core characteristics of the Quadrant Model.
- How to identify the quadrant you're in right now.
- Strengths and pitfalls of each persona.
- Real-life examples that make the quadrants memorable.
- A quick self-assessment to map your default.
- A light preview of movement— the how lives in chapter 5.

Before we break these quadrants down, it's important to understand one thing: this model isn't about judgment—it's about orientation. Wherever you find yourself on the grid right now isn't a verdict; it's a starting point. Behavior is simply the visible expression of your mindset and identity under pressure. By naming it, you give yourself leverage. From here forward, the goal isn't to criticize how you respond—it's to recognize it early enough to choose a better path forward.

Understanding the Structure of the Quadrant Model

"...think about what you can control and solve the problem you can solve with the wisdom you have gained from both your victories and your defeats in the past."
David Mahoney

PRS Behavioral Quadrant Model Detailed

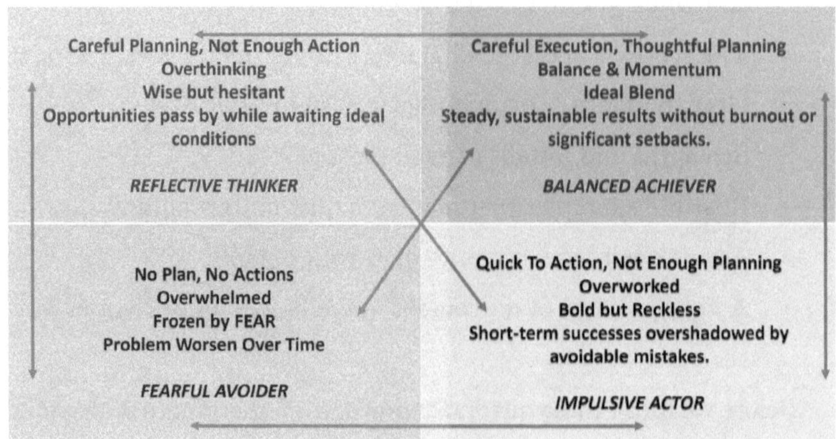

Illustration 12

While the first couple of chapters prepared your mentality and attitude to create balance and momentum in your life, this chapter synthesizes these elements through the quadrant model, enhancing your balance and momentum. It shows the varying degrees of effort between planning and action. It highlights the tendencies you're most likely to fall into, the loops those tendencies create, and the outcomes they produce when you face problems, challenges, and change.

When I first sketched this on paper, it was after yet another late-night spiral — too many ideas, too little progress. I drew two lines, one vertical and one horizontal, to make sense of why I kept over-doing or under-doing. I noticed two things.

- The **horizontal line** represents **reflection** — from low to high.
- The **vertical line** represents **action**— from low to high.

Where those two forces intersect, they form four distinct quadrants — four ways people typically respond when faced with problems, challenges, or change. Each quadrant embodies a relatable persona. Some people are more prone to act; some to hesitate: some overthink; others leap. Neither side is inherently good or bad and it's about recognizing where you are and learning how to shift when needed. This leads to the four quadrant personalities:

- **The Fearful Avoider**: Overwhelmed, frozen by fear or uncertainty.
- **The Reflective Thinker**: Wise but hesitant, stuck in planning mode.

- **The Impulsive Actor**: Bold but reckless, rushing without thinking.
- **The Balanced Achiever**: The ideal blend—thoughtful, strategic, and decisive.

No quadrant is good or bad in isolation. Each has strengths that serve specific scenarios—and predictable traps that stall progress. Your goal isn't to live in a single quadrant forever; it's knowing where you are and navigating on purpose.

Before you begin, choose one particular problem, challenge, or change to take on. If you're dealing with multiple problems or challenges, consult the quadrant model separately for each scenario. Every situation demands its unique approach and can have distinct outcomes.

For example, if your goal is a salary increase at your current job, say a 10% increase, two distinct paths may arise. Seeking an internal promotion or finding a new position elsewhere. While both paths address your initial problem, they necessitate entirely different approaches within the quadrant model, each yielding distinct outcomes.

Another example: consider a strained relationship. You know it needs attention, but are you starting from a place of open communication or long-standing resentment? The same intention—to repair or improve the relationship—requires very different actions depending on where things currently stand. Understanding your starting point determines the level of effort, patience, and reflection required.

In the next four sections, we will look at each of the personality types including their characteristics, examples of behaviors, ideal use cases, and a case study for each. The quadrant model doesn't define who you are—it reveals how your identity responds when pressure shows up. Awareness here gives you choice before habits take over.

The Fearful Avoider: Low Action/Low Reflection Oriented

"If you choose to not deal with an issue, then you give up your right of control over the issue and it will select the path of least resistance."
Susan Del Gatto

The Fearful Avoider is characterized by individuals resisting action and planning because of anxiety, doubt, or fear of making the wrong choice. This avoidance often exacerbates problems. Doubt and uncertainty paralyze them, leading to a cycle of avoidance that can make problems grow worse.

The Fearful Avoider isn't lazy or weak. In many cases, this person is sensitive, thoughtful, and risk-aware, able to see consequences others can't. That awareness can be a strength when it leads to careful choices and self-protection. But when fear takes over, that same awareness turns into hesitation, shutdown, and avoidance. The goal in PRS isn't to eliminate caution—it's to convert caution into small, safe action so the problem stops growing in the dark.

Characteristics:

- Paralyzed by fear, doubt, or anxiety about failure or change.
- Avoids both planning and taking action.
- Often overwhelmed by the scale of the problem.
- May experiences guilt or shame for inaction, which feeds the cycle.

Examples of Behavior:

- Ignoring health symptoms because of fear of a diagnosis.
- Avoiding tough conversations in relationships or the workplace.
- Letting bills pile up because of money anxiety.
- Procrastinating on starting a goal due to fear of judgment or failure.
- Saying "I don't know where to start" and doing nothing.

Use Cases:

- Long-term situations where careful pacing matters (e.g., lifestyle changes).
- Scenarios where small wins and mindset shifts are needed first.
- Situations best approached with support systems (mentors, therapists, planners).
- A valuable starting point for building self-awareness and slowly gaining confidence.

Case Study – Tina, the Overwhelmed Nurse

Tina works night shifts, takes care of aging parents, and has credit card debt growing each month. Ignoring mounting bills and unopened mail, she feels paralyzed by exhaustion and guilt, knowing she needs help but doesn't know where to start. She cancels plans, avoids conversations about her stress, and spends hours scrolling on her phone to numb the pressure.

Her first win isn't a master plan—it's a micro-step that restarts motion. Tina is deep in the Fearful Avoider quadrant. Her stress response is shut down. She needs small, manageable steps to re-engage.

Tina doesn't need a full life overhaul. She needs a reset—a way to break inertia without adding pressure. Her first PRS move is to reduce the problem to one controllable action. She sets a 10-minute timer, opens just the top three envelopes, and writes only what's due and when. No payment plan yet. No shame spiral. Just facts.

Next, she makes one support-based move: she texts a trusted friend and says, "I'm overwhelmed and I need help staying accountable this week." Then she chooses one momentum micro-win for the next few days: five minutes a day organizing mail into two piles—urgent and can wait.

That small sequence doesn't solve everything, but it changes her position. Tina goes from shutdown to motion. And once she's moving again, she can begin the next step of PRS—building clarity, creating a simple plan, and learning how to stay steady under pressure instead of disappearing when life gets heavy.

Avoidance isn't a character flaw—it's often an identity protecting itself from perceived threat. Awareness is the first step toward reclaiming motion.

The Reflective Thinker: Low Action/High Reflection Oriented

"When faced with a problem you do not understand, do any part of it you do understand and then look at it again."
Robert Heinlein

Here, we meet the Reflective Thinker. This persona excels at deep thought and careful planning but delays action indefinitely even when progress is possible because they are always seeking the "perfect" solution.

The Reflective Thinker isn't indecisive or incapable. In many cases, this person is wise, strategic, and able to see angles others miss. Their strength is clarity through thinking. But when reflection has no boundary, it turns into hesitation, perfectionism, and delayed decisions. In PRS, the goal isn't to stop thinking—it's to pair thinking with timed action so momentum can begin.

Characteristics:

- Highly analytical and thoughtful.

- Prone to overthinking and hesitation.
- Prefers to research and plan thoroughly before taking action.
- Fears making the wrong decision, so often delays taking any.

Examples of Behavior:

- Makes extensive pros and cons lists but struggles to decide.
- Revises plans frequently without execution.
- Consumes information (books, podcasts, etc.) without applying it.
- Waiting for the perfect time to start something.
- Miss opportunities due to delays in decision-making.

Use Cases:

- Problems that require deep thinking, strategy, or multiple scenarios.
- Planning for future changes or long-term transitions.
- When initial analysis and risk assessment are vital.
- Research-heavy decisions like investing, relocation, or career change.

Case Study – David, the Aspiring Author

David dreams of writing a novel. He's spent years attending workshops, reading craft books, and outlining ideas. He has notebooks filled with scenes, characters, and world-building. But he never feels ready enough to begin the first draft. He revises chapter one endlessly and never reaches chapter two. He avoids feedback because he's afraid his work isn't good enough yet.

David's strength is thinking—but his progress is slipping. He's trapped in planning without action, the hallmark of the Reflective Thinker. His perfectionism has become his safety blanket. Thinking is a tool, not a destination.

David doesn't need a better plan. He needs boundaries. His first PRS move is to time box reflection and force a small action. He sets a 20-minute timer and writes a "messy draft" of one scene without editing. When the timer ends, he stops. No rewriting. No fixing. He simply creates forward motion.

Next, he makes a support move: he sends that one scene to a trusted friend or writing group with one small and clear request— Give me one thing that works and one thing to improve. Then he chooses a micro-win for the week: write 200 words a day, even if it's bad. Especially if it's bad. The point isn't quality yet—the point is traction.

That small shift changes David's position. He moves from endless thinking to controlled action. And once he proves to himself that imperfect action is survivable, confidence follows. The clarity he was waiting for doesn't arrive before writing—it arrives because of writing. That's how the Reflective Thinker moves toward balance.

Reflection becomes a strength when it leads to movement. When identity values certainty over progress, insight must be paired with action to regain momentum.

The Impulsive Actor: High Action/Low Reflection Oriented

"...we have all, at some point, confused doing something—anything—with actually solving the problem."
Sherry Thomas

The Impulsive Actor is characterized by quick, energetic action. These individuals move fast and decisively, often jumping into situations without slowing down to plan or reflect. While their drive can generate short-term wins, the lack of structure often leads to avoidable mistakes, wasted effort, and burnout.

The Impulsive Actor isn't reckless by nature. In many cases, this person is bold, courageous, and willing to act when others freeze. Their strength is momentum. They bring energy, confidence, and movement to situations that would otherwise stall. But when action isn't guided by reflection, momentum turns into chaos. In PRS, the goal isn't to slow them down—it's to add just enough structure so their effort compounds instead of resets.

Characteristics:

- Quick to act, often without thinking things through.
- High energy and decisive, but lacking in planning.
- Sensation-seeking thrives in urgent environments.
- Struggles with follow-through and long-term vision.

Examples of Behavior:

- Blurting out answers before questions are finished.
- Interrupting others frequently in conversations.
- Buying expensive items on a whim.
- Making career or relationship changes suddenly.
- Reacting emotionally rather than rationally under stress.

Use Cases:

- High-pressure situations where time is extremely limited.
- Emergencies where hesitation could be costly.
- Scenarios that require immediate momentum to break paralysis.

Case Study – Marcus, the Aspiring Entrepreneur

Marcus is passionate and full of energy. He has dozens of business ideas and finally quits his 9-to-5 job to launch a mobile car detailing service. Excited to move fast, he skips market research, orders expensive equipment, and launches before validating demand. He doesn't track expenses or set up a proper invoicing system. Within a few months, cash flow problems emerged. Frustrated, Marcus pivots to a new idea without finishing what he started.

Marcus thrives on action, but his lack of planning and follow-through holds him back. This is the Impulsive Actor in motion—high energy, low structure. His engine is powerful, but there's no steering wheel.

Marcus doesn't need less ambition. He needs a pause with a purpose. His first PRS move is to insert reflection before execution—slowing just enough to clarify what problem he's solving, how small a test he can run before committing fully, and what success looks like in the short term rather than the distant future.

Next, Marcus adds one structure-based support: he tracks expenses weekly and commits to finishing one phase of his business before starting another. His momentum micro-win is simple—one focused action per day that supports the current goal, not a new idea.

That small shift changes everything. Marcus doesn't lose speed—he gains direction. His actions became intentional instead of reactive. Over time, his confidence grows not from constant movement, but from completed cycles. This is how the Impulsive Actor begins moves toward balance—by keeping the engine, but finally adding a steering wheel.

Speed feels productive when identity equates motion with control. The goal isn't less action—its action guided by awareness.

The Balanced Achiever: High Action/High Reflection Oriented

"The wise person devotes more time to structuring problems by considering potential consequences before acting. This leads to better judgments, better foresight, and to behavior that increases the probability of desired outcomes, or decreases the probability of undesired outcomes."
Moshe F. Rubinstein

The Balanced Achiever represents individuals who combine thoughtful preparation with consistent, timely action. They know when to pause and reflect, and when to move forward. Progress doesn't feel rushed or stalled—it feels steady, intentional, and sustainable.

The Balanced Achiever isn't someone who has everything figured out. In many cases, this person has simply learned—through experience—how to recover quickly, adjust calmly, and stay grounded under pressure. Their strength is integration. But even balance requires awareness. Without reflection, balance turns into autopilot. Without action, it turns into stagnation. In **PRS**, balance isn't a permanent state—it's something you continuously recalibrate.

Characteristics:

- Combines thoughtful planning with timely, consistent execution.
- Knows when to pause, reflect, and when to act.
- Adapts well to changing conditions without losing sight of the goal.
- Maintains discipline, clarity, and emotional steadiness.

Examples of Behavior:

- Sets clear goals and follows through with regular check-ins.
- Adjusts strategy mid-way based on new data or outcomes.
- Balances effort, rest, and reflection to avoid burnout.
- Weighs options carefully, then commits and follows through.
- Maintains progress even when motivation fluctuates.

Use Cases:

- Complex or medium-term problems that require consistency and flexibility.
- Projects that demand both planning and persistence.
- Lifestyle changes such as health, finances, or personal development.
- Leadership roles that require direction, empathy, and adaptability.

Case Study: Janelle, the Corporate Project Manager

Janelle leads a product development team at a mid-sized tech company. She's responsible for launching a new feature by the third quarter, when unexpected staffing changes and tight deadlines threaten the timeline. Instead of panicking or forcing unrealistic expectations, she breaks the project into milestones, builds in buffers, and communicates clearly with her team.

As new challenges arise, Janelle adjusts the plan without losing momentum. She checks in regularly, makes small course corrections, and protects her team's energy by balancing urgency with sustainability. The feature launches on time, slightly under budget, and receives positive user feedback.

Janelle represents the Balanced Achiever—not because everything went perfectly, but because she stayed responsive without becoming reactive. Balance, in this sense, isn't perfection; it's timing. Knowing when to pause, when to push, and when to recalibrate is what allows progress to continue without burning out the system.

Balance isn't a fixed state—it's an ongoing practice. Identity stays healthy here only when awareness prevents comfort from turning into stagnation.

Assessing Your Quadrant

"You can't reach your destination if you don't know where you're starting from."
Unknown

The quadrant model goes beyond theory, offering practical and meaningful insights. By identifying your current quadrant, you gain awareness of your default tendencies, enabling actionable steps toward balance. Whether facing significant life changes, daily decisions, or persistent obstacles, applying the quadrant model guides you toward intentional and effective solutions. Before you can move forward, you must first identify where you are starting from. Ask yourself:

- Am I taking any action at all, or am I stuck thinking and waiting?
- Do I feel confident in what I'm doing, or am I reacting emotionally?
- Do I keep researching or planning but never begin?
- Am I overwhelmed, afraid, or avoiding the situation entirely?

Your honest answers drop a pin on your current location. From there, the route forward becomes clearer. Recognizing your quadrant is awareness; moving between them is growth. The next step of this system—covered in the following chapter—shows how to do that movement through a structured process called the 4A Framework: Anticipate, Activate, Advance, and Achieve. For now, remember this: Every problem begins in one quadrant and resolves in another. The journey from fear to balance, from hesitation to confident action, is not linear—it's cyclical, adaptive, and deeply human.

Personally, I naturally lean toward being an Impulsive Actor. When faced with challenges, my instinct is immediate action. Often without thorough preparation. For example, when building a custom bar at home, based solely on a few YouTube tutorials, I enthusiastically jumped into the project, neglecting careful measurement and planning. My excitement led me to measure once and cut twice. Although I ultimately completed the bar, the results required extra effort and patchwork. Had I paused briefly to integrate some aspects of the Reflective Thinker, the project would have gone more smoothly, efficiently, and aesthetically. This experience vividly illustrated the importance of balanced planning and action. To this day there are still uneven parts on the bar.

Recognizing your default responses and proactively working toward balanced action is transformative. The quadrant model equips you with self-awareness, clarity, and practical guidance to turn problems into meaningful opportunities, moving steadily toward your personal and professional goals. You can't solve a problem if you don't know how you're approaching it.

The quadrant model doesn't just help you understand yourself. It helps you make your next move. By naming where you are, you reclaim the power to change your direction. And from there, actual progress begins. This model transforms us by revealing who we are, where we're getting stuck, and how to move forward with clarity and purpose.

The next chapter introduces the 4A Framework—the roadmap that transforms awareness into motion, showing you how to move between quadrants with clarity, consistency, and control.

The quadrant model helps you recognize your behavioral default—where you are starting from, what holds you back, and how to pivot with purpose. By naming your tendencies, you reclaim control. This model transforms awareness into motion, guiding you from confusion to clarity, from reaction to response, and from chaos to deliberate progress. Identifying your quadrant isn't about judgment, it's about awareness. You might be a Balanced Achiever in your professional life but a Fearful Avoider when it comes to your health. You might move from one quadrant to another in a single week. That's normal. This book isn't asking you to be perfect. It's asking you to be honest. Once you know where you are, you can learn how to shift intentionally and strategically toward balance.

The quadrant you start in matters—but it's not the destination. Each quadrant reflects how you respond when identity, pressure, and awareness collide. The goal isn't to live in the Balanced Achiever permanently; it's to recognize where you are and move intentionally. In the next chapter, we'll focus on how movement actually happens—how awareness turns into momentum through deliberate action.

Find Your Quadrant

"The wise see failure as feedback and adjustment as progress."

This practice is designed to take 10–15 minutes total. Don't overthink your answers. Remember: balance isn't about staying centered at all times; it's about *returning* to center faster. Every quadrant shift is a chance to practice awareness and intentional motion—the heart of the PRS Model. Understanding your behavioral quadrant is about building awareness—not judgment. The goal isn't to label yourself; it's to observe your default mode so you can move with intention instead of reaction. This short exercise will help you recognize your current quadrant, identify patterns, and practice small, strategic shifts toward balance.

Step 1 – Map your default by reflecting on a recent challenge or stressful decision. Then answer honestly and see which statement feels most true and identifies your current quadrant of behavior.

- Did I **avoid** it out of fear or uncertainty?
- Did I **overthink** it, waiting for the perfect moment?

- Did I **rush in** without a clear plan?
- Or did I **balance** reflection and action effectively?

Step 2 – Awareness is your steering wheel—when you know how you drive, you can start correcting courses. For the next seven days, observe your patterns. Record each time you face a problem, big or small. In your notes, mark which quadrant you operated from. At the end of the week, look for trends:

- Do I spend most of my time in one quadrant?
- What triggers make me shift to another?
- What time of day or environment pushes me off balance?

Step 3 – Calibrate your compass. The goal is movement *with awareness*, not perfection. Every adjustment counts. Once you recognize your default, apply a micro-adjustment:

- **Fearful Avoider:** Take one small action within 24 hours.
- **Reflective Thinker:** Set a 15-minute timer and act before it expires.
- **Impulsive Actor:** Pause to write down one short plan before proceeding.
- **Balanced Achiever:** Check your rhythm—are you pushing or pacing too hard?

Step 4 – If you leaned too heavily toward avoidance, overthinking, or impulsiveness, create an accountability mirror. Write one sentence about what you'll do differently tomorrow. Small reflections build powerful awareness. Each evening, ask yourself:

"Which quadrant did I live in today, and what did it cost or create?"

Step 5 – Create shifts in real time. That short pause break's reaction loops and puts you back in control—right in the Balanced Achiever Lane. When emotions spike or pressure builds, take one deep breath and say quietly:

"Pause. Reflect. Adjust."

KEY INSIGHTS FOR CHAPTER 5

- **The quadrant model builds awareness, not judgment.** It helps you recognize how you actually respond to problems, challenges, and change—so you can move with intention instead of reaction.

- **Your starting quadrant matters more than your goal.** Progress depends less on what you want to solve and more on how you're approaching it in the moment.

- **Time pressure influences behavior.** Different quadrants emerge depending on urgency, stress, and emotional load. Knowing this helps you choose a response instead of defaulting to habit.

- **Self-awareness is the steering wheel.** By observing your patterns over time, you can identify triggers, environments, and conditions that push you into avoidance, overthinking, or impulsiveness—and correct sooner.

- **Balance is not a permanent state—it's a skill.** You're not meant to live in one quadrant. Mastery comes from recognizing when you're off-center and returning to balance faster.

- **Small adjustments create real change.** Micro-shifts—pausing, acting sooner, slowing down, or planning briefly—interrupt reaction loops and restore control in real time.

- **Each quadrant reflects a common human response:**

  - *The Fearful Avoider* hesitates due to fear or overwhelm.

- o *The Reflective Thinker* overanalyzes and delays execution.

- o *The Impulsive Actor* acts quickly without enough structure.

- o *The Balanced Achiever* integrates reflection and action for steady progress.

- **Every quadrant has strengths and risks.** No quadrant is "bad." Problems arise when you stay in one too long. Awareness allows you to leverage strengths while avoiding predictable pitfalls.

- **The Balanced Achiever is not perfection—it's alignment.** Thoughtful preparation combined with timely, consistent action produces sustainable momentum over time.

- **The goal of PRS is intentional movement.** When you pause, reflect, and adjust, you regain agency. Problems stop controlling you—and start informing your next move.

Framework & Momentum

"It is not the strongest of the species that survives, nor the most intelligent—it is the one most adaptable to change."
Charles Darwin

Knowing where you are is powerful, but knowing how to move is transformational. In the last chapter, we explored the quadrant model, understanding the four mindsets that shape our reactions giving each persona a name, a face, and a set of behaviors and we saw how each type responds to problems, challenges, and change. Awareness of these patterns gives you clarity. But awareness alone doesn't shift behavior. While the quadrant model reveals where you are, the 4A Framework teaches you how to move forward from there—intentionally, not reactively.

Think of the quadrant as rooms in a house. You may find yourself in the basement (Fearful Avoider), wanting to get to the living room (Balanced Achiever), but unsure which steps to take. Maybe you're always jumping from task to task (Impulsive Actor), but you want to slow down and become more intentional. Or perhaps you're stuck in overthinking mode, and need to take your first courageous step forward.

That movement requires a framework. You need a mechanism — something that helps you take what you've discovered about yourself and turn it into forward motion. That's where the 4A Framework —**anticipate**, **activate**, **advance**, and **achieve**—comes in. The 4A Framework is a simple but powerful structure for movement. It's the movement engine of the PRS system. It doesn't tell you what to think—it shows you how to move. It turns insight into action, intention into traction, and effort into momentum. Identity influences which stage you resist, which one you rush, and which one you avoid sustaining—awareness helps you move through each with intention.

Most people don't get stuck because they lack motivation or discipline. They get stuck because they're trying to do everything at once—or applying the right tools at the wrong time. Reflection when action is needed. Action when clarity is missing. Pushing forward without a map. Resting without direction.

The PRS components were never meant to be applied all at once. They align naturally with the stages of movement in the 4A Framework. Think of the 4A Framework as the sequence of movement, and the PRS components as the tools you apply inside each phase. Mission, mindset, momentum, maintenance—each has a role, but only when introduced at the right moment. When these elements are misaligned, progress feels chaotic and exhausting. When they're aligned, movement feels intentional and sustainable.

This chapter shows you how that alignment works. First, you'll learn the 4A Framework itself—how movement actually happens and why it's cyclical, not linear. Then, you'll see how the PRS components integrate into each stage of 4A, so you're using the right tool at the right time. Finally, we'll layer the quadrant model back in, showing how your behavioral posture influences how you move through each phase—and how to adjust when progress stalls.

From personal experience and years of helping others, I've learned that people don't change quadrants just because they want to. They change when they understand where they are, what phase they're in, and how to move forward intentionally from there.

I've had to do this repeatedly—during military deployments, through loss and recovery, while raising six kids, and while navigating high-stakes leadership roles. Every breakthrough came from the same process: awareness, aligned movement, and adjustment. Not perfection. Not brute force. Just the right move at the right time. That's what this chapter is designed to give you—not just insight, but forward motion. Here's what we'll explore:

- Movement is your framework and momentum is the engine — it's what turns insight into traction and awareness into sustained progress.
- How the 4A Framework works in real life.
- How PRS components plug into each 4A stage, so you use the right tool at the right time.
- How your quadrant affects movement—and what to do when you stall, rush, or freeze.
- How to build momentum without chaos, burnout, or perfectionism.

The goal isn't to stay in the Balanced Achiever quadrant forever. That's unrealistic.

The goal is to recognize where you are, move intentionally, and return to balance faster each time. That's how momentum is built. That's how progress becomes sustainable. And that's where real change begins.

Movement isn't about speed—it's about direction sustained over time. The 4A Framework exists to keep you moving intentionally, even when progress feels slow or uneven.

4A Framework: Movement with Intention

"We always hope for the easy fix: the one simple change that will erase a problem in a stroke. But few things in life work this way. Instead, success requires making a hundred small steps go right – one after the other."
Atul Gawande

Movement with intention is what separates progress from burnout. Most people aren't stuck because they don't care or aren't trying hard enough — they're stuck because they're moving without a framework or waiting for certainty that never arrives. The 4A Framework gives you permission to stop forcing outcomes and start responding intelligently to where you actually are.

When movement is intentional, you don't waste energy fighting yourself. You don't jump ahead when you need clarity, and you don't overthink when action is required. Each step has a purpose, and each phase earns its place. That's what turns effort into momentum and momentum into lasting change.

Every challenge or goal will bring you through the four stages, sometimes quickly, sometimes over months. Each one has its own rhythm, lessons, and traps. Learning to recognize which stage you're in keeps you from getting stuck. The 4A Framework shows you how to move, and the quadrant model shows you how you tend to move. As you prepare for your problem, challenge, or change, you may shift back and forth between personas. The movement itself isn't what matters most—it's the self-awareness that comes with it. That awareness helps you recognize your typical behavior and learn how to counter or leverage it, turning weaknesses into strengths.

The beauty of 4A is that it's cyclical, not linear. Each stage represents a critical phase in your journey. You'll go through this framework over and over in different areas of life. You might be in Advance with your career but stuck in Anticipate in your health. And that's okay. Whether you're tackling a personal goal, rebuilding after failure, or facing a life change that has you paralyzed, the framework is both flexible and grounded. The point is not to race to the top but to keep moving forward. You just need to know where you are and what to do next. Let's break it down.

PRS 4A Framework

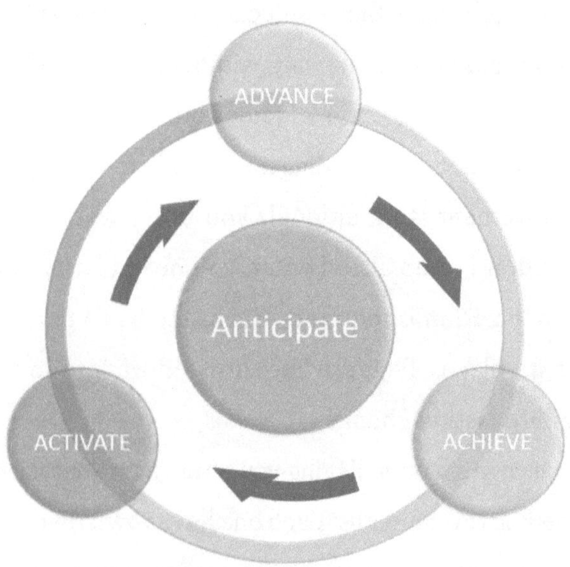

Illustration 13

Step 1 Anticipate – Prepare for the Journey

This is where you pause, assess, and prepare through self-reflection to gain clarity and understand the terrain before taking action. Here, you clarify your why, identify potential roadblocks, and visualize success. You take inventory of your tools, time, and support system. Anticipation builds readiness; it's not waiting—it's strategic patience. Many people skip this part because they crave results, but skipping preparation only guarantees backtracking later.

Anticipation isn't hesitation—it's preparation. When done with intention, it prevents wasted motion later.

Common Pitfall: Over-planning without transition. Anticipation is meant to prepare you for action—not replace it. When reflection doesn't lead to a clear first step, it turns into hesitation. Pause just long enough to ensure your energy is aimed at the right target. Pitfalls don't mean failure—they're signals. When noticed early, they help you recalibrate instead of restart.

Activate – Take Courageous Action

Activation is not about perfection—it's about momentum. This is where courage meets motion. You'll face resistance here—self-doubt, hesitation, distractions—but pushing through creates the spark for progress. Start small. Movement builds confidence, and confidence compounds.

Activation doesn't require confidence—it creates it. Movement, even imperfect movement, breaks inertia.

Common Pitfall: Mistaking motion for progress. Without a clear direction set during anticipation, action becomes noise. Activation works best when the target is already defined.

Advance – Build Consistency and Adaptability

Advancing means maintaining pace and adjusting intelligently. You've already started moving; now you refine. The goal is consistency—not speed. Identify what's working, adapt to feedback, and strengthen your discipline. This is the grind stage, where persistence turns small wins into sustainable momentum.

Advancement is where most progress is built—not through intensity, but through consistency and adjustment.

Common Pitfall: Expecting constant motivation. Success here depends on habits and systems, not emotion.

Achieve – Sustain and Evolve

This stage isn't about finality—it's about sustaining progress, consolidating growth, and evolution. Achievement isn't the end; it's a checkpoint. Celebrate your progress, and look ahead to the next evolution by reviewing lessons learned, sharing your growth with others, and preparing for the next cycle. Every achievement feeds the next anticipation—just at a higher level of mastery.

Achievement isn't an ending—it's a checkpoint. Every arrival prepares you for the next cycle of growth.

Common Pitfall: Stagnation. Achievers sometimes mistake rest for regression. True achievement includes reflection and renewal.

When people say they feel stuck, overwhelmed, or burned out, it's usually because they're activating without anticipating, advancing without mapping, or achieving without maintaining. The framework helps you diagnose where you are — and which tools actually belong there.

When you first apply the 4A Framework, it might feel awkward—like learning a new instrument. You'll hesitate, over-adjust, or swing between extremes. That's normal. Each pass through the cycle strengthens self-awareness.

Start by identifying a single issue or goal—something specific but meaningful. Run it through the stages consciously. Notice when you stall, when you rush, and when you feel balance. The process itself will reveal which quadrant you default to. Over time, the framework becomes second nature—your internal operating rhythm for solving problems, overcoming challenges, and managing change.

Seasoned practitioners of PRS don't just react to problems—they anticipate them. They use reflection strategically, act deliberately, and adapt quickly. Mastery looks less like intensity and more like rhythm. Over time, you stop shifting quadrants emotionally and start shifting them strategically. You'll transition smoothly based on logic and experience versus reacting emotionally.

As a Balanced Achiever, you'll revisit reflection to analyze results, shift into action to implement changes, and repeat the cycle intentionally. Even fear becomes useful—it signals where preparation or courage is needed next. True mastery is not balance achieved but balance maintained. Understanding the stages of movement is only half the equation. The next question is what to focus on during each stage— because not every tool belongs everywhere.

The Science of Motion

"I can calculate the motion of heavenly bodies,
but not the madness of people."
Sir Isaac Newton

Everything in life is in motion. Our thoughts, emotions, and decisions are constantly shifting, creating ripples that shape what happens next. Even when you feel stuck, motion still exists — it just might be going in circles. There's always something moving beneath the surface: our choices, our mindset, our energy. The PRS system brings structure and awareness to that movement to help you turn that unconscious, random motion into meaningful momentum and intentional progress.

This isn't a new idea. It's the same truth that governs the universe. In the late 1600s, the father of modern physics, Sir Isaac Newton, defined and published his *Three Laws of Motion*, the foundation of classical physics. Though he was describing how objects move, his principles mirror how people grow. Change, progress, balance — all follow the same universal laws of motion. PRS builds on that same universal truth: motion creates outcomes—and outcomes create feedback.

Illustration 14

Newton's First Law – The Law of Inertia

An object at rest stays at rest, and an object in motion stays in motion unless acted upon by an external force.

In physics, inertia is the natural resistance of an object to any change in its state of motion. A stationary object will remain still, and one already moving will continue to move at the same speed and direction unless an external force acts upon it. For example, a parked car won't roll forward until someone pushes it — and once it's moving, it won't stop until friction or brakes apply an opposite force.

In life, inertia shows up as hesitation, fear, procrastination, or burnout — that feeling of being mentally parked while life keeps moving around you. We stay in the same routines, the same mindsets, and even the same problems because no new force has acted on us yet. The PRS system provides the external force of awareness which breaks the standstill by helping you identify where you are, what's holding you back, and what needs to move first.

Once inertia is broken and motion begins, stopping becomes equally difficult. Growth becomes natural. Progress becomes the default. And no setback, distraction, or external resistance can easily stop you from fulfilling your goals and living your purpose.

The Law of Inertia explains why awareness and mindset are the foundation of every component. Without awareness —the external force —, the mission, motive, and method remain ideas on paper. Once that spark of recognition hits — the realization that you can move — the engine starts. The mindset becomes your initial push, the model helps you steer, and the momentum keeps you accelerating forward. Every time you apply the PRS, you're overcoming your own inertia — turning stillness into movement, confusion into clarity, and potential into progress.

Newton's Second Law – The Law of Acceleration

Force equals mass times acceleration (F = ma).

In physics, acceleration describes how quickly an object changes its motion when force is applied. The greater the force on an object — or the lighter its mass — the faster it accelerates. A car moves quicker when you press harder on the gas pedal, and a lighter vehicle will respond faster than a heavy truck given the same push.

In everyday life, acceleration represents how quickly we move once effort meets intention. When you set a clear goal and apply focused energy, things start to shift. For example, a person who commits to daily progress — writing one page, saving one dollar, or exercising for ten minutes — begins to accelerate faster than someone waiting for motivation to appear. Every deliberate push compounds momentum, turning slow progress into measurable speed.

The Law of Acceleration explains how effort, mindset, and structure combine to generate growth. Your motive and mindset act as the driving force; they determine the strength and consistency of your push. The method provides the structure that directs that energy so it doesn't scatter. The model keeps you aware of when to apply more force or ease up, while the momentum transforms each push into sustained velocity. This is where progress shifts from slow movement to true acceleration — when clarity meets consistent effort. The more aligned your energy is with your purpose, the faster your results appear, and the easier it becomes to break through life's resistance.

Newton's Third Law – The Law of Action and Reaction

For every action, there is an equal and opposite reaction.

This law describes how forces always come in pairs. When one object pushes against another, both experience an equal force in opposite directions. A rocket launches upward because its engines push exhaust gases downward; a swimmer moves forward by pushing water backward. Every movement creates a mirrored response in the opposite direction.

In life, this principle plays out through the chain reactions created by our decisions and behaviors. Every action—every word, effort, or choice—sets energy into motion that comes back in some form. Speak kindness and it echoes in trust. Delayed action and consequences build quietly in the background. When you push toward growth, life pushes back with resistance, but that resistance is also feedback—it shapes strength and awareness.

The Law of Action and Reaction represent the ongoing dialogue between intention and result. Your mission sets the direction of force, while your motive determines its depth and persistence. Each time you act—whether by applying a new strategy, shifting mindset, or recalibrating your model—the world responds. That response becomes data, reflection, and feedback. The model (your steering) helps interpret the reactions, the 4A Framework converts that feedback into forward motion, and your tools and maintenance refine the process so you can course-correct without losing speed.

Action and reaction in the PRS aren't opposites—they're a rhythm. Every setback, obstacle, or unexpected pushback isn't failure; it's information. The system teaches you to absorb those reactions, reflect on them, and redirect with greater precision. Over time, you stop fearing resistance and start using it. That's when you shift from surviving motion to mastering it. Just like gravity keeps planets in orbit, awareness keeps your life's trajectory balanced and centered. Motion is universal—but mastery, that's intentional.

Aligning the PRS Components to the 4A Framework

"There is a time in the life of every problem when it is big enough to see, yet small enough to solve."
Mike Leavitt

One of the biggest sources of confusion in personal growth systems isn't effort—it's sequencing. People try to clarify their mission while they're already overwhelmed, build momentum without direction, or focus on maintenance before anything meaningful has been built. The PRS components solve that problem by aligning what you focus on with where you are in the process.

While the 4A Framework provides the movement sequence—anticipate, activate, advance, achieve. The PRS components plug into that sequence, giving each phase the right tools at the right time. Instead of applying every concept at once, you work with a focused set of priorities that match the stage you're in. This alignment turns effort into progress and prevents burnout, drift, or false starts. What follows is a practical map showing how each PRS component fits naturally into the 4A Framework—so you're not just moving, but moving with intention.

4A Framework & PRS Components

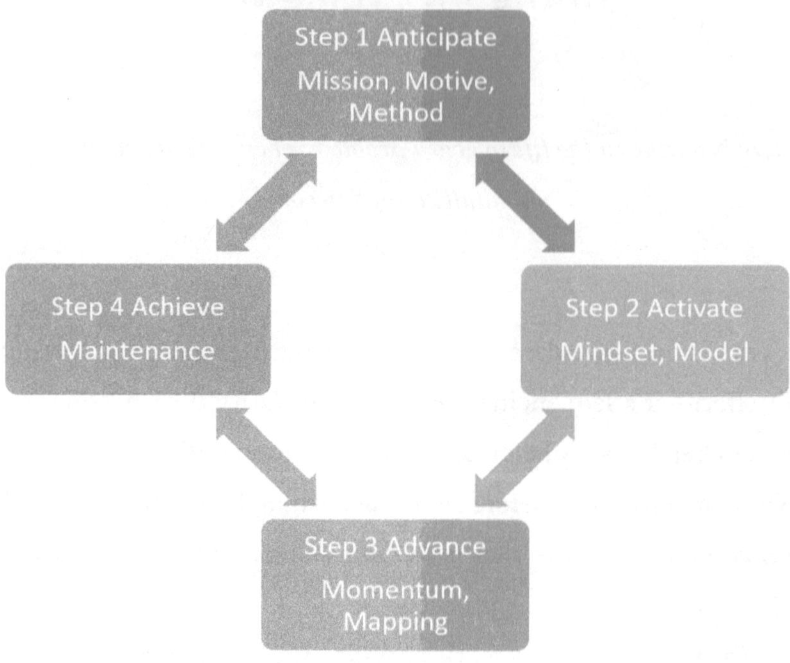

Illustration 15

Anticipate → Mission, Motive, Method

This is the preparation stage. Before action makes sense, you need direction. Mission clarifies where you're going. Motive explains why it matters. Method outlines how you'll approach the problem. When people rush past this stage, they often act with energy but without alignment.

Activate → Mindset, Model

Activation is where thinking turns into motion. Mindset determines whether fear, confidence, or doubt drives behavior. The Model — especially the Quadrant Model — helps you recognize how you're showing up while you act. Activation without the right mindset leads to burnout or impulsiveness. Activation with awareness creates traction.

Advance → Momentum, Mapping

Once movement begins, consistency matters more than intensity. Momentum keeps you moving when motivation fades. Mapping helps you adjust when conditions change. This is where many people stall — not because they failed, but because they didn't adapt. Advance is about staying in motion while recalibrating.

Achieve → Maintenance

Achievement isn't the end — it's stabilization. Maintenance protects what you've built. This includes time management, task management, risk awareness, recovery, and renewal. Without maintenance, progress decays. With it, momentum becomes sustainable.

Seen this way, PRS is not a checklist—it's a sequence. It's a system you move through — again and again — applying the right components at the right time. Each component has a job, and that job depends on where you are in the movement. Using the right tools at the right stage makes progress feel focused instead of overwhelming. When they're used out of order, even good effort creates friction. This alignment helps you answer a simple but powerful question: What should I be focusing on right now? Not everything—just the components that belong to the phase you're in.

Once the components are properly aligned, movement becomes clearer. But clarity alone doesn't guarantee effectiveness. How you show up during each phase—your behavioral tendencies, reactions, and default patterns—still determines how smoothly you move forward. That's where the quadrant model comes in.

Aligning the Quadrant Model to the 4A Framework

"All problems become smaller when you confront them instead of dodging them."
William F. Halsey

The 4A Framework moves forward like time—anticipating, activating, advancing, and achieving. But how effectively you move through each stage depends on the behavioral quadrant you're operating from in that moment. When progress stalls, it's rarely because the framework failed—it's because the wrong behavioral posture is being applied to the current stage. The quadrant strategies that follow are designed to help you realign your behavior so you can continue moving forward through the 4A process—returning to the Balanced Achiever state as efficiently and sustainably as possible.

Imagine you set aside four hours to clean four rooms. One room per hour. Simple. In the first room, you start as a Reflective Thinker. You're thorough. You wipe the same surface three times. You reorganize drawers. You aim for perfection. Forty-five minutes pass, and only a third of the room is done. At that moment, awareness kicks in. Time is now the constraint — not quality.

To stay on track, you intentionally shift quadrants. You move into Impulsive Actor mode. You stop re-cleaning. You wipe once instead of three times. You finish the room by the one-hour mark. Once momentum is restored, you recalibrate again. In the next room, you operate as a Balanced Achiever. Two wipes instead of three. No rushing, no perfectionism. Clean enough, on time.

Nothing about the task changed. What changed was how you moved. This is PRS in action. You didn't abandon standards. You adjusted behavior to meet reality. That's what effective and efficient problem-solving looks like in real life. The goal isn't to eliminate impulsiveness or overthinking. The goal is to know when each one serves the moment. Balance isn't doing everything perfectly — it's doing the right amount at the right time. Effective problem-solving requires knowing when to slow down for quality and when to speed up for completion.

Knowing your quadrant is powerful—but movement requires more than awareness. It demands strategy, self-awareness, and intentional action. Strategic movement between quadrants is not about fixing who you are, it's about adapting how you respond. The right strategy, applied at the right time, can transform stagnation into progress and fear into focused action. Once again don't aim to be perfect, aim to be intentional.

Below are focused strategies for each quadrant, designed to help you either stabilize within it or move toward a more effective quadrant depending on the situation. Whether you're feeling stuck or striving to evolve, these targeted approaches offer direction.

The strategies are designed around behavioral tendencies, not rigid stages. Each quadrant has predictable strengths and traps, and these strategies help stabilize or redirect movement regardless of where you are in the 4A Framework. That said, they work best when paired with awareness of your current stage—anticipating when you need clarity, activating when you need momentum, advancing when consistency matters, and achieving without stagnation. Think of these strategies as behavioral adjustments that help you move more effectively through any phase.

4A Framework & Quadrant Model

	Step 1 Anticipate	Step 2 Activate	Step 3 Advance	Step 4 Achieve
Fearful Avoider	Anticipate	Activate	Advance	Achieve
Reflective Thinker	Anticipate	Activate	Advance	Achieve
Impulsive Actor	Anticipate	Activate	Advance	Achieve
Balanced Achiever	Anticipate	Activate	Advance	Achieve

Illustration 16

The Fearful Avoider

Fearful Avoiders are not lazy or incapable. They are often overly cautious, sensitive, and deeply aware of risk. They tend to see consequences clearly and care deeply about making the right choice. This awareness can be a strength—until fear overwhelms movement.

When uncertainty feels too heavy, reflection turns inward and stalls. Action feels unsafe, so problems are postponed in hopes they resolve on their own. Over time, avoidance compounds stress and reinforces self-doubt—not because the person lacks ability, but because fear has replaced forward motion.

In PRS, the Fearful Avoider doesn't need pressure—they need psychological safety and a way to get back into motion without overwhelm.

Strategies:

- Name the Fear: Labeling fear separates it from identity and reduces its power.
- Start Tiny: Micro-actions restore momentum without triggering shutdown.
- Visualize Success: Mental rehearsal builds confidence before action.
- Seek Support: Accountability reduces isolation and increases follow-through.
- Track the Wins: Evidence of progress weakens the fear narrative.

The Reflective Thinker

Reflective Thinkers are thoughtful, analytical, and future-oriented. They excel at planning, risk assessment, and seeing multiple angles of a problem. Their strength lies in thinking before acting—a critical skill in complex or high-stakes situations.

The challenge arises when reflection becomes endless. The desire for certainty delays action, and planning turns into protection from potential failure. Progress stalls not from lack of insight, but from waiting for conditions that feel safe enough to begin.

In PRS, the Reflective Thinker doesn't need more information—they just need to act even imperfectly.

Strategies:

- Break It Down: Small actions bypass analysis paralysis.
- Seek Clarity: Identify whether fear, doubt, or missing data is the real blocker.
- Create a Reward System: Reinforce execution, not just planning.
- Set Boundaries on Reflection: Time-box thinking so action has space to occur.

The Impulsive Actor

Impulsive Actors are energetic, decisive, and action-oriented. They thrive in urgency and are often the first to move when others hesitate. Their willingness to act creates momentum and can break stagnation quickly.

The downside appears when speed replaces strategy. Action without reflection leads to wasted effort, preventable mistakes, and burnout. The problem isn't too much action—it's action without alignment.

In PRS, the Impulsive Actor doesn't need to slow down completely—they need a steering wheel, not a brake.

Strategies:

- Pause and Reflect: A brief check-in prevents reactive decisions.
- Create a Plan: Even minimal structure multiplies effectiveness.
- Prioritize and Focus: Fewer actions, executed well, outperform scattered effort.
- Use Time Delays: Short waiting periods reduce emotional reactivity.

The Balanced Achiever

Balanced Achievers are effective, disciplined, and grounded. They combine thoughtful planning with consistent action, which allows them to produce results without chaos or burnout. Their strength lies in rhythm—knowing when to push, when to pause, and when to adjust.

However, balance still requires awareness. When results come easily or routines become automatic, a Balanced Achiever can drift—not into failure, but into comfort. This isn't complacency by default; it's a loss of intentional urgency. Progress continues, but growth may slow if goals aren't revisited or challenged.

In PRS, balance is not a destination—it's a practice. The Balanced Achiever's work is not to do more, but to stay aligned, alert, and willing to evolve as conditions change.

Strategies:

- Set Clear, Evolving Goals: Define what success looks like now—and revisit it regularly.
- Commit to Consistency: Routines are your best friend. Habits compound into momentum.
- Monitor Progress: Use journals or habit trackers to visualize your growth. Regular check-ins help maintain motivation and alignment.
- Challenge the Comfort Zone Intentionally: Growth happens at the edges of comfort, not in disruption—push with purpose, not pressure.

Example: Striving for Financial Independence

"You have to change your thinking if you desire to have a future different from your present."
Germany Kent

Let's take the following example as a composite case designed to illustrate how the PRS system works in real life. It shows how clarity, momentum, and balance are built—not through perfection, but through intentional movement using the quadrant model and the 4A Framework. The details may feel familiar, because the patterns are. Here's what it looks like when the 4A Framework guides momentum—and how quadrant shifts either block or support each stage.

John and Sarah both worked full time and earned decent incomes, yet every month felt tight. Bills arrived faster than progress, and despite steady effort, they never seemed to get ahead. Financial independence—having choice, margin, and peace of mind—felt like something meant for other people. Over time, fear crept in. They stopped looking closely at their budget, convinced they were already too far behind to fix things.

They weren't irresponsible. They paid their bills and talked often about wanting financial independence—not a specific number, just the ability to breathe. Less stress. More margin. Fewer late-night arguments about money. But they began to realize that wanting change and moving toward it are not the same thing.

For a long time, they operated without awareness or clarity. They felt the weight of the problem but avoided looking directly at it. Bank apps stayed unopened. Credit card balances went unchecked. The size of the unknown felt safer than confronting the facts. This wasn't laziness—it was the Fearful Avoider showing up in the Anticipate stage, where reflection turns into paralysis instead of preparation.

Eventually, discomfort turned into urgency. They decided to just do something. Subscriptions were canceled overnight. Grocery spending was slashed. Extra hours were picked up. For a few weeks, activity felt productive—exhausting, but productive. Yet nothing felt stable. Every decision was reactive. Progress was inconsistent. Momentum kept collapsing. They hadn't failed at activation—they had activated from the Impulsive Actor quadrant. Lots of motion. Very little direction. That's when they paused—not to quit, but to recalibrate.

Instead of chasing fixes, they returned to planning and reflection. Together, they defined what financial independence actually meant to them: reduced stress, predictable cash flow, and the ability to handle setbacks without panic. They reviewed their budget—not to solve everything, just to understand the terrain. Fear didn't disappear, but it became manageable once it had boundaries.

With awareness built and clarity restored, they re-entered activation—this time deliberately. One priority. One card. One behavior change at a time. No dramatic overhauls. Just aligned action.

As weeks passed, their focus shifted from intensity to consistency. They built simple routines. Monthly check-ins replaced emotional reactions. When progress slowed, they adjusted instead of abandoning the plan. This was Advance—where discipline replaces motivation and balance becomes a practice, not a goal. Momentum returned quietly.

Months later, they weren't working harder—they were working smarter. Reflection and action reinforced each other. When stress spiked, they knew how to pause. When momentum dipped, they knew how to restart. They had moved into the Balanced Achiever quadrant, not by staying there permanently, but by learning how to return to it faster. They truly were on their way to financial independence.

Financial independence doesn't arrive overnight. But clarity replaced chaos. Momentum replaced frustration. Balance replaced burnout. They didn't just improve their finances—they learned how to move through problems without losing themselves in the process. What ultimately changed wasn't their income; it was learning how to move through anticipation, activation, advancement, and achievement without letting fear or impulse take over the process.

Movement without navigation eventually leads to exhaustion. The 4A Framework gives you motion—but motion alone isn't enough. In the next chapter, we'll focus on mapping: how to track progress, adjust direction, and reroute without losing momentum when life pushes back.

Build Your Momentum

"Little by little, a little becomes a lot."

This practice is designed to take 10–15 minutes total. Don't overthink your answers. Progress compounds like interest. Each micro-action fuels momentum until the engine of change runs on its own power. Keep turning the key—motion creates mastery. Momentum is rarely built through massive leaps. It's the quiet discipline of showing up, recalibrating, and restarting faster each time you stall. Use this exercise to put the 4A Framework into action and transform awareness into motion. Each step is designed to help you move forward intentionally— no matter your starting point.

Step 1 – Anticipate

This step reinforces that clarity comes before action. You are intentionally resisting the urge to activate before you're aligned. Anticipation creates preparedness, and preparedness prevents paralysis. Every week, ask yourself "What could stop my progress this week?" List the top 3 potential obstacles—time, fear, distractions, or fatigue—and write one small countermeasure for each.

- Example: *If I get overwhelmed → I'll take a 5-minute pause to breathe and reset.*

Step 2 – Activate

This step is about acting with awareness—not intensity—so momentum is built, not forced. Action generates clarity. Waiting for the perfect moment kills momentum. Write down several micro-actions you could take and complete one that aligns with your goal. Circle one micro-action and do it today—before you plan the next one.

Step 3 – Advance

This step shifts focus from motivation to consistency, where real momentum is sustained. Once motion begins, consistency keeps it alive. Pick one daily ritual that moves you closer to your target and commit to seven consecutive days. Here are some ideas:

- Journal 5 minutes each morning.
- Read two pages of this book nightly.
- Plan tomorrow before bed.
- Track your streak and reflect: *What got easier by Day 7?*
- Remember—advancement is discipline, not drama.

Step 4 – Achieve

This step protects progress by preventing drift, burnout, or premature restarting. Celebrate progress, not perfection. Every mile you drive counts toward mastery. At the end of the week, measure results. Ask:

- What did I actually complete?
- What did I learn about my rhythm?
- What would make next week's "engine" run smoother?

Bonus Exercise – The Restart Ritual

You don't lose the miles you've already driven. You simply shift gears and keep moving. Whenever you lose momentum, don't start over—restart smarter. Use this quick mantra to reengage:

"Pause. Reflect. Adjust. Activate."

KEY INSIGHTS FOR CHAPTER 6

- **Movement requires more than awareness.** Insight shows you where you are; intentional action is what changes your trajectory.

- **The 4A Framework gives you a repeatable way to build momentum.** Anticipate, Activate, Advance, and Achieve keep progress moving without chaos or burnout.

- **Anticipation is not hesitation—it's strategic preparation.** When you identify obstacles early, you reduce fear and prevent wasted effort later.

- **Activation creates clarity you can't think your way into.** One aligned action is often enough to break inertia and reveal the next step.

- **Advancement is built through rhythm, not intensity.** Consistent micro-actions compound into real momentum over time.

- **Achievement is a checkpoint, not the finish line.** Reflection turns results into lessons, and lessons feed the next cycle of growth.

- **Momentum breaks down when sequencing breaks down.** Using the right tool at the wrong time creates friction, even when your intentions are good.

- **PRS components are phase-specific.** When you match the component to the stage, effort becomes focused and sustainable.

- **Your quadrant affects how you move through every stage.** Awareness lets you adjust behavior so you don't stall in fear, loop in analysis, or sprint into burnout.
- **PRS is the human translation of motion.** Newton described how force creates movement; PRS shows how clarity and action create progress.

Approaches & Applications

"In any moment of decision, the best thing you can do is the right thing, the next best thing is the wrong thing, and the worst thing you can do is nothing."

Theodore Roosevelt

Decision-making is the engine that drives everything you've learned so far. The quadrant model helps you recognize where you are; the 4A Framework shows you how to move. But when it comes to choosing your next move—when fear, doubt, or urgency creep in—it all comes down to one thing: the quality of your decisions.

Decision-making is one of those areas where people get stuck the most. Sometimes we over analyze until the moment passes. Other times, we rush in without thinking through the consequences. Both extremes can keep us from moving forward. What we need is not just a single way to decide, but a set of strategies we can pull from depending on the situation. Think of this as a decision-making toolbox.

Some people freeze, others rush, and many bounce between the two. The goal of this chapter isn't to give you one "right" way to decide—it's equipping you with a toolbox of strategies you can pull from depending on the situation. Think of it like the **PRS** in motion You pause, assess, act, and adjust through the power of choice.

Not every decision requires deep analysis. Sometimes, it's as simple as asking why something keeps happening—or deciding, once and for all, yes or no. Other times, structured frameworks help you slow down, think clearly, and weigh outcomes more effectively. This chapter brings it all together. It's where awareness meets action, and where hesitation turns into momentum. Here is what we'll explore:

- Mapping your approach to reroute when obstacles appear.
- Recognizing the hidden biases that quietly distort our decisions.
- Six approaches to making meaningful and actionable forward movement.
- Getting to the root of decision making with the Five Whys.
- Using the Yes/No Philosophy and cutting out maybe.

Mapping doesn't eliminate wrong turns—it makes them useful. When you track where you are honestly, even setbacks become information instead of failure.

Understanding the Nature of Decisions

"You will only be remembered for two things:
the problems you solve or the ones you create."
Mike Murdock

Every action or reflection starts with a decision. Whether you're stuck in fear, stuck in thought, acting impulsively, or moving with balance, it all hinges on the decision to move. We make some decisions on autopilot; others stop us in our tracks. The key is learning which decisions deserve thought, and which ones don't.

Big decisions don't always need big approaches. Sometimes it's as simple as asking why something keeps happening? Or just simply saying yes or no. Other times, you need a rational checklist, an ethical lens, or an incremental pilot. Decision-making is a toolbox but, the skill is knowing which tool to grab when.

When I tackle big decisions, time and task management are the most important aspects to keep in mind. What time frame am I taking into consideration? For example, buying a car and buying a house have massive differences. You can probably go through the whole car- buying process within a week, while buying a house can sometimes take a full year. Task-wise, for this example, you would need to secure financing through cash in hand or get a loan, and this could have many steps depending on my credit score.

This chapter aims to unpack what decision-making really is, why it's so hard for some and easy for others, and how to improve this skill using both practical tools and internal clarity.

At its core, decision-making is the cognitive process of choosing between options to solve a problem or seize an opportunity. Decisions can be deliberate or automatic, logical or emotional, big or small, but they all influence our path.

Hidden Biases That Quietly Shape Our Decisions

Before we choose a path, we need to know whether our internal map is accurate. It is important to be aware that some factors affect our decision making whether or not we want them to. We don't make logical decisions and then feel them. We make emotional decisions and justify them later with logic.

These come from some biases that most often cause people to feel first, decide second, and justify later. Acting as mental shortcuts, these biases can help our brain quickly process complex information, yet they can cause distorted thinking. These skewed perceptions of reality can lead to failure to consider all available evidence. This is not an all-inclusive list, but some of the most common.

1. **Loss Aversion**. We fear losing what we have more than we value gaining something better. This keeps people stuck in jobs, relationships, and habits they've outgrown.
2. **Sunk Cost Fallacy**. We continue because of what we've already invested—time, money, energy—even when it no longer serves us.
3. **Confirmation Bias**. We look for information that supports what we already believe and ignore what challenges it. This reinforces blind spots and slows growth.
4. **Status Quo Bias**. We prefer familiar discomfort over unfamiliar improvement. Change feels risky—even when staying put costs more in the long run.

5. **Social Proof**. We follow what others are doing to feel safe or validated, even when their path isn't right for us.

6. **Overconfidence Bias**. We overestimate what we know or how well things will go, leading to poor preparation and preventable mistakes.

7. **Availability Heuristic**. We judge risk based on what's most recent, vivid, or emotional—not what's most likely or accurate.

8. **Negativity Bias**. Negative experiences carry more weight than positive ones, shaping decisions through fear instead of balance.

9. **Planning Fallacy**. We underestimate time, effort, and cost, assuming things will go smoother than they usually do.

10. **Outcome Bias**. We judge decisions by how they turned out, not by whether the decision itself was sound at the time.

The following biases aren't flaws or failures. They're common mental shortcuts that influence nearly every human decision. Awareness doesn't eliminate them—but it gives you a choice. These biases don't disappear with experience. I catch myself falling into them—just faster than I used to.

I see the sunk cost fallacy when I play poker. I've stayed in hands longer than I should have—not because the odds were good, but because I had already invested too much to walk away. That same pattern shows up in real life when we keep investing in decisions that no longer make sense, such as confirmation bias when doing research for business or investments.

Decision Making Breakdown

"I know but three classes of men: those who see the whole, those who see but a part, and those who see both together."
Johann Caspar Lavater

Every decision we make—whether conscious or instinctive—shapes our progress. The key to mastering problem re-solving is learning how to decide effectively and when to apply the right approach. Not every situation requires deep analysis or lengthy reflection. Depending on the situation, you'll need logic, intuition, or the courage to move forward with good enough instead of chasing perfection.

This section breaks down several established decision-making approaches and how they can be applied within the PRS to improve clarity, movement, and outcomes. Each one has its strengths, weaknesses, and ideal use cases. The goal isn't to master just one—it's understanding how to use the right one at the right time. Faster Capital lists six Decision making models: Choosing the Right Path: Exploring Decision making Models below and what they are typically used for.

The Rational Approach– Step by Step

The Rational Decision-Making Approach is the most structured and analytical of them all. It relies on logic, data, and reason to evaluate choices. You define the problem, gather information, generate alternatives, weigh pros and cons, make a choice, and then evaluate the results. It's clean, methodical, and rooted in facts rather than feelings.

In the PRS, this thrives in the Reflective Thinker and Balanced Achiever quadrants—where deliberate thought and planning guide action. It's ideal when you have time to analyze, when stakes are high, or when measurable outcomes are required. For example, when deciding whether to switch careers, this helps you map the decision through objective factors like financial stability, skill alignment, and growth potential rather than emotion alone.

The Behavioral Approach– Psychology Matters

The Behavioral Approach acknowledges that humans aren't purely logical beings. Emotions, biases, and experiences play a huge role in how we make choices. This approach considers the why behind the what—why we choose certain paths, repeat certain patterns, or avoid specific risks.

In the PRS, this connects deeply to the Fearful Avoider and Reflective Thinker quadrants, where hesitation or overthinking may stem from psychological barriers rather than lack of knowledge. The quadrant model asks us to pause and understand those internal influences—our fears, biases, motivations, and the environments that shape them. For example, a manager hesitant to delegate may not lack trust in their team—it may stem from a subconscious fear of losing control. Recognizing that bias allows better, more balanced decisions.

The Ethical Approach– Doing the Right Thing

Some decisions aren't just about efficiency or results—they're about values. The Ethical Decision-Making Approach centers on moral reasoning and doing what aligns with personal or organizational integrity, even when it's inconvenient. This approach asks key questions: Who will this decision impact? Is it fair? Does it uphold my principles? Sometimes, the best decision isn't the most profitable or comfortable one—it's the one you can live with long after the outcome.

In the PRS, this is essential for those in leadership roles, guiding others or representing something larger than themselves. It aligns with the Balanced Achiever, who must weigh results with responsibility.

For example, a leader discovers a mistake in reporting that no one else has noticed. Ethically, the right move is to address it transparently, even if it costs short-term favor.

The Intuitive Approach– Trust Your Gut

Not every choice allows for analysis. Sometimes, the best guide is your gut. The Intuitive Decision-Making Approach emphasizes instinct—the inner voice formed from experience, pattern recognition, and subconscious processing. This shines in high-pressure environments where you must act fast with incomplete data.

In the PRS, it lives in the Impulsive Actor quadrant, but at its best, it draws on wisdom, not recklessness. True intuition isn't guessing; it's rapid recognition built from experience. For instance, a security engineer may sense that a system issue "feels off" before seeing the logs. Or a parent may sense something's wrong with their child without being told. Those instincts come from deep, often unseen, mental decisions built over time.

The Incremental Approach– Small Steps, Big Wins

The Incremental Decision-Making Approach believes progress doesn't have to happen all at once. Instead of massive leaps, it's about taking small, calculated steps—testing, adjusting, and improving as you go. This fits perfectly within the Advance phase of the 4A Framework and supports the Balanced Achiever mindset. It's ideal for complex or uncertain problems where moving in small, controlled increments builds confidence and insight.

Think of it like driving through fog. You don't stop until it clears—you move carefully, adjusting your speed and direction as visibility improves. The same applies to business, health, or relationships: you make a decision, evaluate, adjust, and advance again.

The Satisfying Approach– Good Enough is Great

The Satisfying Approach challenges perfectionism. Instead of waiting for the perfect option, you choose the one that's "good enough" to meet your goals. This doesn't mean lowering standards—it means recognizing when more analysis won't add more value.

In PRS, this helps Reflective Thinkers break free from analysis paralysis. Sometimes, the search for the "perfect" solution delays progresses indefinitely.

The Satisfying approach helps you decide, act, and move forward. For example, choosing between two qualified job candidates. Both are capable, but one is available sooner. Instead of over analyzing every variable, you hire the one that meets your needs now and start building momentum.

Decision-Making Techniques

"There's no such thing as running away from the problem. They're very patient and will wait a lifetime for you."
Darnell Lamont Walker

The Five Whys Technique Uncovering Root Cause

Sakichi Toyoda, the Japanese industrialist, inventor, and founder of Toyota industries, Developed the concept for Five Whys in the early 1900s. After his death, this concept was formalized into the Toyota Production system (TPS). The Five Whys is a simple yet powerful technique for quickly uncovering the root cause of a problem by repeatedly asking "why?" when facing recurring issues.

Often, surface-level symptoms mask deeper issues that, if resolved, would prevent the recurring problems. The Five Whys technique is an easy-to-use method that helps you quickly through systematic questioning. It helps identify the root cause of a problem and understand how one process can cause a chain of other problems.

This technique can be used for simple, moderate, and difficult problems. More complex problems may require this method in combination with others. Especially when problems involve human factors or interactions. Follow these steps to apply the 5 Whys technique.

1. Clearly define your problem statement.
2. Ask "why" the problem occurs, noting the answer clearly.
3. Continue asking "why" each subsequent answer occurs.
4. Typically, after approximately five iterations, you will reveal the underlying root cause.

Example: Our team missed a critical deadline.

1. **Why?** We underestimated the work required.
2. **Why?** We didn't properly scope the project.
3. **Why?** We rushed the planning process.
4. **Why?** We started late because of previous project delays.
5. **Why?** We didn't prioritize projects correctly.

By clearly identifying the root cause, poor project prioritization in this example, you can directly address the actual issue rather than treating only symptoms.

Yes/No Guide to Better Decisions

Every decision matter, especially when facing critical problems. A simple Yes/No decision-making guide can streamline this process, ensuring decisions align with your values, priorities, and long-term objectives. When facing a decision, ask yourself:

- Does this align with my core values and principles?
- Will this positively affect my primary goals?
- Is the potential reward greater than the risk involved?
- Am I prepared to accept responsibility for the outcome?

Evaluate your responses:

- If most answers are yes, the decision is likely beneficial and aligns well with your objectives.
- If most answers are no, carefully reconsider or seek alternatives.
- A balanced mix of yes and no requires deeper analysis. Consider additional information, seek advice, or weigh the pros and cons carefully.

Example:

You're considering a career-changing job offer. Using the Yes/No guide, you might reflect:

- Does it align with your values? *(Yes)*
- Does it support your goals and career growth? *(Yes)*
- Does it support your career growth? *(Yes)*
- Do the benefits outweigh the risks? *(Yes)*

- Are you ready to accept the responsibility and changes involved? *(Yes)*

With predominantly yes answers, the decision clearly aligns positively with your long-term goals. Tools don't replace judgment—they sharpen it. Mapping helps you slow down just enough to choose direction instead of reacting to pressure. Navigation keeps momentum alive when conditions change. Without mapping, movement turns into drift. With it, you can adjust course without losing confidence or direction.

Decision to Execution: Can Do, To Do, Will Do, Do

"The future depends on what you do today."
Mahatma Gandhi

Understanding decisions is essential, but clarity alone does not produce progress. At some point, awareness must translate into structured action.

While refining my own mapping approach, I discovered that my grandfather, George L. Germain, had written about success decades earlier using a simple progression: **Can Do. To Do. Will Do. Do.** The sequence struck me in its simplicity. It mirrored something I had been building in my own way.

Many decision tools help prioritize tasks by distinguishing what is urgent from what is important. This progression focuses on something deeper: turning clarity into sustained execution. His framework emphasized motivation and disciplined action. PRS expands on that foundation by adding behavioral awareness and recalibration, but both share the same underlying truth — clarity must move.

Can Do – Awareness of Strengths

"Can Do" begins with inventory. It is the process of recognizing your knowledge, skills, experiences, character, and personal tendencies. Before pursuing any goal, you must understand what you already possess. You cannot build effectively if you do not know your materials.

In PRS language, this aligns with identity and clarity. It asks: Who are you right now? What strengths are available to you? What patterns shape your responses under pressure? Progress begins with honest awareness.

To Do – Planning With Intention

"To Do" moves awareness into structure. It transforms vague hopes into defined objectives and converts desire into direction. Written goals create clarity, and timelines create focus. Planning becomes the bridge between intention and movement.

My grandfather referred to this as creating a MAP — My Action Plan. In modern language, this resembles SMART objectives: Specific, Measurable, Attainable, Relevant, and Time-bound. Within PRS, this represents the shift from reflection to movement. Awareness without planning drifts; planning channels energy.

Will Do – Inner Commitment

"Will Do" is where intention becomes personal. Skill and planning mean little without commitment. This stage reflects the internal decision to follow through, especially when excitement fades and difficulty rises. It is the choice to continue when progress slows and outcomes are uncertain.

In PRS terms, this is motive in motion — alignment between identity and direction. It is the quiet resolve that sustains effort when no one is watching.

Do – Action and Effort

Finally, there is "Do." This stage moves beyond theory, intention, and preparation into consistent action. Execution requires effort, adjustment, repetition, and persistence. It demands engagement with reality rather than reliance on inspiration alone.

Success rarely arrives through motivation by itself. As Thomas Edison famously suggested, achievement is far more perspiration than inspiration. Action transforms structure into progress.

My grandfather, George L. Germain, was not simply a casual writer. He earned a degree in psychology, authored five books, spoke at conferences, and worked as a teacher and consultant. His work centered on discipline, structured thinking, and personal responsibility. Long before I consciously articulated PRS, he was teaching principles of awareness, planning, commitment, and execution.

His breakdown of Can Do, To Do, Will Do, Do was clear and practical. It emphasized inventory, planning, belief, and action. That foundation stands on its own. It reflects decades of study and experience in understanding how people think, decide, and act.

What struck me most was not that our ideas were identical — they are not — but that they were aligned in spirit. His work focused on disciplined pursuit and structured motivation. PRS builds upon that foundation by adding behavioral awareness, recalibration, and sustainable navigation under pressure.

Both approaches converge on a simple and enduring truth: progress requires movement. Yet how we move — and how aware we are while moving — determines whether that progress strengthens us or exhausts us.

If his framework emphasized execution, PRS emphasizes conscious navigation. One generation clarified the essence of success. The next expands it into a structured system for navigating problems, change, and complexity. In honoring his contribution, I'm not replacing it. I'm continuing it.

Master Your Decisions

*"The path is made clear not by the light ahead,
but by the step you take now."*

This practice takes 10–15 minutes. Don't overthink it. Clarity comes through motion. Every decision is a steering adjustment — some minor, some life-altering. When you navigate with intention instead of reaction, uncertainty loses its power. Use this exercise to move from confusion to clarity in real time.

Step 1 – Name the Crossroad. You cannot navigate a decision you haven't defined. Naming it activates awareness. Write one decision currently weighing on you.

- Example: *Should I leave my current job for a new opportunity?*

Step 2 – Use the 5 Whys. Ask "*Why?*" five times to uncover the root cause of your hesitation. Continue until emotion becomes logic. The fifth "why" often reveals the real issue beneath the surface.

Example:

1. Why am I unsure about leaving my job? → I'm afraid of losing stability.
2. Why do I fear that? → Because I've been in survival mode before.
3. Why does that still affect me now? → I haven't defined what stability means today.
4. Why haven't I defined it? → I keep focusing on comfort instead of growth.
5. Why do I want growth now? → Because comfort no longer challenges me.

Step 3 – Apply the Yes/No Philosophy. Rewrite the decision as a direct question and answer honestly. If both choices create discomfort, choose the one aligned with your mission and long-term growth. Clarity is not always comfortable. Growth rarely is.

- If I say *yes*, what do I gain—and what do I risk?
- If I say *no*, what do I protect—and what do I lose?

Step 4 – Define the Criteria for "Right." Before making any final choice, ask the questions below. If these align, your internal navigation system is calibrated. Now pause and assess where you stand in the progression of action: Do you clearly understand what you can do? Have you defined what you need to do? Are you fully committed to doing it? Or are you hesitating before execution?

1. Does this decision align with my **mission**?

2. Does it honor my **motive and identity**?

3. Does it fit within my current **method and capacity**?

Step 5 – Execute & reflect. Make the decision and observe the outcome. Every result provides feedback. Even detours offer direction. Ask:

- Did this decision move me closer to balance or further from it?

- Which bias if any might be influencing how I interpret the result?

KEY INSIGHTS FOR CHAPTER 7

- **Decisions are the engine of movement.** Every shift in clarity, balance, or momentum begins with a choice. The quality of your decisions determines the quality of your progress.

- **There is no single right way to decide.** Effective PRS requires flexibility. Different situations demand different decision-making approaches based on time, risk, emotion, and impact.

- **PRS transforms decision-making from reaction to navigation.** Instead of freezing or rushing, you learn to pause, assess, act, and adjust with intention.

- **Perception shapes choice before logic ever enters the picture.** Emotions, assumptions, and mental shortcuts often influence decisions long before tools or frameworks are applied.

- **Awareness restores control.** When you recognize biases and emotional distortions early, they lose their ability to quietly steer your decisions.

- **The Rational Approach strengthens clarity.** Logic, structure, and evaluation are powerful when time allows and stakes are high.

- **The Behavioral Approach reveals hidden drivers.** Fear, bias, and past experience often influence decisions more than facts. Awareness restores control.

- **The Ethical Approach anchors integrity.** Decisions aligned with values create long-term stability, trust, and self-respect—even when they cost something in the short term.

- **The Intuitive Approach has value when grounded in experience.** Instinct becomes an asset when paired with reflection rather than impulse.

- **The Incremental Approach sustains momentum.** Small, deliberate steps reduce risk and build confidence when outcomes are uncertain.

- **The Satisficing Approach breaks paralysis.** Choosing "good enough" prevents perfectionism from stalling progress.

- **The Five Whys technique exposes root causes.** Asking "why" repeatedly shifts decision-making from surface symptoms to core issues—preventing repeat problems.

- **The Yes/No Philosophy simplifies complexity.** Clear criteria reduce emotional noise and align decisions with mission, motive, and method.

- **PRS in Practice reinforces decisiveness through action.** Naming the decision, uncovering root causes, applying Yes/No clarity, and executing with reflection turns uncertainty into direction.

- **Clarity comes through movement, not overthinking.** Decisions don't require certainty—they require alignment.

- **Every decision is feedback.** Whether the outcome succeeds or fails, it provides data that improves your next choice.

- **Mastery is not perfect judgment—it's faster course correction.** The goal isn't to avoid mistakes, but to recognize them sooner and adjust with confidence.

Tools & Techniques

"Give me six hours to chop down a tree and I will spend the first four sharpening the axe."
Abraham Lincoln

When faced with a problem, most people jump straight into action and grab whatever idea, advice, or instinct pops into their head. But as you've likely already discovered, charging into battle without a plan often leads to wasted time, energy, and frustration. That's why before we go any deeper into the heart of problem re-solving, we need to stop and sharpen the axe.

This chapter is about preparation. The right mindset is critical, yes, but without the right tools and techniques, it's like trying to build a house with your bare hands. You need strategies that help you work smarter, not just harder. You need methods that help you manage your time, focus your energy, and make clear decisions when chaos threatens to cloud your thinking.

Think of this chapter as your toolbox. Inside are the foundational tools and mental frameworks I've relied on throughout my professional life in the military, cybersecurity, and business, and in my personal life as a father and husband. These are the things that help me stay grounded, efficient, and productive, even when life throws curveballs from every angle.

But here's the catch. You don't need to master, or use, all of the tools in this chapter at once. Pick the tools that match your current problem. Some situations call for discipline and a daily routine. Others require deep reflection or structured planning. The point isn't perfection; it's progress. Having the right tools ready gives you more confidence and control when it's time to act. Over time, what you maintain becomes part of who you are—identity reinforced through repetition, not intention alone.

You'll also notice that many of the techniques in this chapter apply not just to fixing problems, but to preventing them. In the cybersecurity world, we call this risk mitigation. In life, it's simply about being proactive. In this chapter, we'll cover:

- Maintaining balance and being ready for the long haul to reach your destination (goals).
- Mastering new skills through practice and mindset.
- Performing a SWOT analysis to analyze your strengths and weaknesses in the context of the opportunities and threats that you may face.
- Setting SMART goals that lead to action instead of being overwhelmed.
- Managing your time like an executive, using a simple mental perspective.
- Prioritizing tasks using tools like the Eisenhower Matrix.

- Thinking about risk with clarity and strategy.
- Using your dreams and rest time for problem re-solving.
- Grounding your thinking in Stoicism to stay calm under pressure.

Each of these tools will help you become more effective, intentional, and resilient. No fluff. Just practical techniques that will give you an edge and whether you're facing a personal crisis, a professional dilemma, or a simple case of procrastination. This chapter isn't about becoming perfect. It's about becoming prepared. Because when you have the right tools and the right mentality, you're no longer just reacting to life; instead, you're building it, one intentional step at a time.

Maintenance isn't about doing more—it's about preserving what works. It's how progress survives beyond motivation. Let's open the toolbox.

Skill Mastery

"It's not that I'm so smart, it's just that I stay with problems longer."
Albert Einstein

Willpower Versus Skill

When I interview or train new cybersecurity candidates, I immediately gauge their willpower and skill levels. Willpower refers to an individual's drive, motivation, and resilience. The internal factors that push someone to engage deeply with a task or challenge. Skill refers to the current abilities and expertise the individual already possesses. Based on my experience, sheer willpower often outperforms initial skill levels, because individuals with strong determination are more likely to seek knowledge proactively, overcome setbacks, and rapidly acquire new skills.

For example, the candidates I've seen succeed quickly in cybersecurity weren't necessarily the ones who started with the strongest technical skills. Instead, they were driven by curiosity, passion, and a relentless desire to learn. This strong willpower propelled them through challenges, accelerated their skill acquisition, and eventually positioned them ahead of peers who relied solely on existing skills or credentials.

10,000 Hours

In the book *Outliers*, Malcolm Gladwell stated it takes 10,000 hours to master anything. That is approximately five years if practicing an average of 40 hours a week. This, of course, is an oversimplification as talent, level of practice, level of commitment, and having a teacher can make a difference. But as a general rule for the average, it is pretty true. Some people need more; some people need less. Learning a language does not really need 10,000 hours, but if you wanted to switch careers, it might.

When I transitioned into the IT cybersecurity industry, I had no education, degrees, certifications, experience, or skills in the field. I received some formal training and mentorships with the Air Force.

Around the five-year mark I started feeling comfortable in my role and could train others. Even with 20 years under my belt, I do not consider myself to be an expert but still learning and growing.

Dunning-Kruger effect

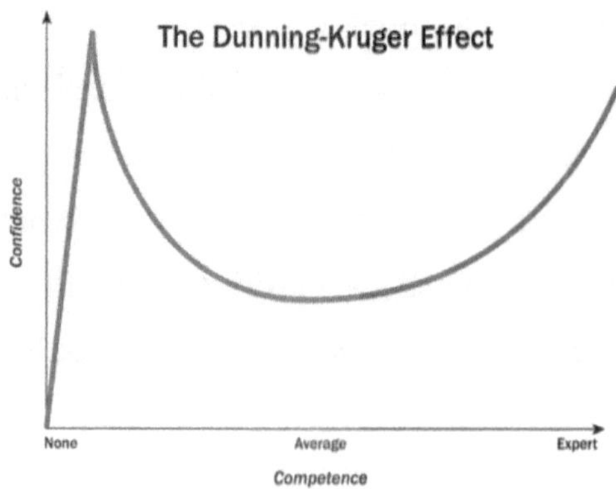

Illustration 17

The Dunning-Kruger effect describes a cognitive bias where individuals with limited knowledge or competence in a domain significantly overestimate their expertise. Essentially, beginners don't possess the perspective needed to realize their knowledge gaps, while experienced individuals may underestimate their abilities because of their awareness of complexities and remaining unknowns. Recognizing this effect can help us remain humble, maintain continuous curiosity, and be open to ongoing learning and feedback as we can all learn something from someone.

Learning, Knowing, and Teaching

To teach something, you have to know it first. To know something, you have to learn it first. There is a clear progression in skill mastery. You must first learn a skill before truly knowing it, and knowing it deeply enough is a prerequisite for teaching it effectively. The true test of mastery is the ability to clearly and confidently transfer knowledge to others. If you struggle to explain or teach something, it's often a sign that you still have more to learn yourself.

Teaching is not merely the sharing of information. It involves breaking down complex ideas, addressing questions confidently, and adapting your communication style to different learners. Each time you teach, you reinforce your own knowledge and gain deeper insights, further solidifying your mastery.

SWOT Analysis

"An unexamined life is not worth living."
Socrates

Illustration 18

Before charging forward, it's important to understand the terrain—
personal or professional. One of the most practical tools for this is a
SWOT analysis, a simple yet powerful framework traditionally used in

business and strategic planning. While it was designed for companies, it's incredibly effective for individuals looking to grow personally, professionally, or emotionally.

SWOT stands for strengths, weaknesses, opportunities, and threats. When applied to personal development, it becomes a mirror that reflects where you excel, where you struggle, what resources or chances are around you, and what might hold you back. This honest self-assessment gives clarity and direction before you commit to major goals or pivot your life in a new direction. Here's how to apply the SWOT framework to your personal life:

Strengths

- What are you naturally good at?
- What skills or habits have helped you succeed in the past?
- What do others consistently praise you for?

Example: You might be highly adaptable in stressful environments. A strength that allows you to remain calm and focused under pressure.

Weaknesses

- What habits or behaviors hold you back?
- Are there emotional blind spots or mindset patterns that cause you to self-sabotage?
- Do you avoid certain responsibilities or hard conversations?

Example: You may lack follow-through on long-term projects, often starting strong but fading because of boredom or distraction.

Opportunities

- What current situations or trends can you take advantage of?
- Are there people, networks, or tools within reach that could help you grow?
- How can you turn a current challenge into a stepping stone?

Example: Maybe a mentor at work will guide you, or a community group nearby can help you build a support network.

Threats

- What external forces or recurring stressors might derail your efforts?
- Are you in a toxic work or personal environment?
- Are procrastination, burnout, or financial instability looming?

Example: You might be in a job that drains your energy and leaves little time for side projects or self-improvement.

When done honestly, a SWOT analysis becomes more than an exercise—it becomes an outline. You can set better goals because you know what to leverage, what to strengthen, what to avoid, and what to protect. Don't be afraid to revisit your SWOT as you grow. You'll be surprised how your answers evolve over time and how empowering that awareness can be.

Before taking on a new customer or project, I like to run a quick SWOT analysis — not just on the work itself, but on myself and the environment I'm stepping into. I look at my own strengths, weaknesses, opportunities, and threats in relation to the customer and their culture. My biggest strengths usually come from my technical expertise and my ability to communicate effectively. My weaknesses revolve around procrastination, especially when dealing with projects that have tight timelines and firm deadlines. Knowing this upfront helps me stay accountable, so I tackle small tasks early to keep momentum. On the opportunity side, I'm always looking for ways to expand my skill set in the ever-changing world of cybersecurity. The biggest threats are burnout and late nights, which can disrupt family balance. Doing this assessment before every major effort gives me clarity and perspective. It helps me anticipate workload, manage stress, and keep both my career and home life in sync.

SMART Goals

"A problem well stated is a problem half solved."
Charles Kettering

Now that you've identified your strengths, weaknesses, opportunities, and threats, it's time to turn those insights into focused action. The next step is defining clear, structured goals that give your strategy direction. Setting goals is essential, but they require thorough planning to be effective and efficient. Many people, when you ask them their goals, say something vague like, "I want to make more money," but without a structured approach, these goals lack direction. The SMART goal system tackles that issue by providing a structured approach to goal-setting, ensuring they are:

- **Specific** – The goal should be clear and well-defined.
- **Measurable** – There should be a way to track progress.
- **Achievable** – The goal should be realistic considering the resources available.
- **Relevant** – The goal should align with broader objectives.
- **Time-bound** – There should be a deadline or timeframe for completion.

Keep in mind that not all goals look the same. Some goals are easy to measure—like saving a specific amount of money or paying off a debt. Others are about improvement—like becoming a better communicator, building confidence, or feeling more balanced at work.

Both types of goals matter. The key is giving each one a clear way to track progress, whether that's through numbers, feedback, or consistent habits. That's where the SMART framework helps—by turning vague intentions into something you can actually work toward. Let's break this down using the SMART goal system:

Specific

Being specific eliminates ambiguity and provides a clear starting point define how you will achieve this. Instead of saying, "I want to make more money" say, I want to make more money by getting a part-time job in retail, freelancing, or selling handmade crafts online."

Measurable

A goal should have measurable progress indicators so you know when you're getting closer to success. Replace I want to make extra income with I want to earn an additional $500 per month from my side job. This allows you to track earnings and adjust your approach if needed.

Achievable

While ambition is great, goals should be realistic and attainable based on available resources and time. If you already work a full-time job, setting a goal of making an extra $10,000 a month immediately may not be practical. A more achievable goal might be: I will commit 10 hours a week to a part-time job or freelance work to generate an extra $500 a month. This makes success more realistic and sustainable.

Relevant

Goals should align with your overall objectives and priorities. If financial security is your primary concern, making more money should contribute to paying off debt, saving for a home, or building investments. A relevant goal might be: I will use my additional income to pay off

$5,000 in debt over the next year, reducing my financial stress and improving my credit score. Ensuring the goal is relevant helps maintain motivation and prevents distractions.

Time-bound

A goal should have a clear deadline to create urgency and accountability. Without a timeframe, goals lack direction and urgency, making it easier to procrastinate. Swap "I will start making extra money soon" with the time-bound goal "I will apply for three part-time jobs within the next two weeks and begin earning extra income by the end of next month." Having a deadline keeps you focused and motivated to take consistent action.

When I started my nonprofit, everything felt overwhelming at first. The vision was big — I wanted to help as many kids as possible — but the steps to get there were blurry. I needed to create a vision, mission and purpose statements. It wasn't until I sat down and applied the SMART goals approach that things began to take shape.

- **Specific:** Start with my local county and eventually build out from there.
- **Measurable:** I will track donations and food drives through monthly reports.
- **Achievable:** I will start small and partner with local businesses and volunteers instead of trying to do everything alone.
- **Relevant:** I made sure it was relevant to the mission — to fight childhood hunger right here in my own community.
- **Time-bound:** I will launch before the end of the year.

Once those five elements came together, everything started moving. What once felt impossible turned into a structured, living mission with real impact. That's when I learned that clarity creates confidence — and that's the real power of SMART goals.

Time Management: As a Maintenance Tool

"We all have 24 hours in a day. Whether rich or poor, young and old. It is what you do with it that really matters. What will you do?"

Unknown

Time management is often framed as a productivity skill—how to do more, faster, with less wasted effort. That framing isn't wrong, but it's incomplete. In the PRS, time is better understood as a maintenance tool. Not for tasks, but for you. How you spend your time reveals what you're sustaining, what you're neglecting, and what direction your life is actually moving—whether you're aware of it or not.

I didn't arrive at this understanding by avoiding hustle. Quite the opposite. Hustle played a major role in shaping me into the problem solver I am today. There were seasons where intensity was necessary—working long hours, taking on multiple responsibilities, pushing through discomfort, and solving problems under pressure. Hustle builds capacity. It sharpens instincts. It creates momentum. But hustle without awareness eventually creates imbalance.

PRS doesn't reject effort. It teaches when to apply it, when to ease it, and when to redirect it. The issue isn't working hard. The issue is living too long inside a single priority while neglecting the others. In PRS, I look at time through three core priorities:

- **Priority 1: Stability and Responsibility.** This includes work, health, family obligations, and commitments that keep life functioning. When Priority 1 is neglected, stress rises fast. Bills pile up. Health declines. Relationships strain. Stability is the foundation—without it, everything else becomes harder.
- **Priority 2: Growth and Future Leverage.** This is where progress is built. Learning new skills. Creating something meaningful. Investing time in goals that don't pay off immediately but compound over time. Priority 2 is often where hustle shows up—and where it belongs—but only when anchored to purpose.
- **Priority 3: Renewal and Connection.** Rest, recovery, joy, relationships, and reflection live here. This isn't "extra." It's essential. Without renewal, even the most driven people burn out, lose clarity, or become reactive instead of intentional.

Balance is not giving each priority equal time every day. That's unrealistic. Balance is ensuring none of them are ignored for too long. There will be seasons where Priority 1 and Priority 2 demand intensity. That's not failure—that's reality. But if Priority 3 disappears entirely, momentum eventually collapses. Likewise, too much rest without responsibility or growth leads to stagnation.

Time, then, becomes a way to maintain alignment across these priorities, not optimize output. It helps you notice when you're over-investing in one area at the expense of the others—and course-correct before burnout or drift sets in. An aligned week might include:

- Responsibilities handled consistently
- Purpose-driven effort that moves you forward
- Intentional space to recover and reconnect

Some weeks will lean harder in one direction. That's fine. What matters is your ability to return to balance faster instead of living in extremes. This is where clarity, balance, and momentum quietly reinforce one another. Clarity helps you see where your time is actually going. Balance keeps any one priority from consuming the system. Momentum comes from sustained movement without self-destruction. This section isn't about doing more. It's about maintaining the conditions that allow you to keep going.

For a long time, my life leaned heavily toward Priority 1 and Priority 2 only. Work, responsibility, growth—those were the focus. Hustle helped me build capacity and solve hard problems, but it also taught me where imbalance shows up when maintenance is ignored.

Today, I don't manage my time to do more—I manage it to stay effective longer. I regularly check which priority is being overused and which one is being neglected, then adjust before burnout or stagnation sets in. The goal isn't perfection. It's catching drift early and correcting course.

In the next section, we'll zoom in further—shifting from how you maintain balance over time to how you decide what to work on next using practical decision tools. Time maintenance sets the boundaries. Task management determines the decisions inside them. One helps you protect your energy and direction; the other helps you prioritize action by urgency and importance. When they work together, you're not just staying busy—you're staying intentional. Be mindful of how you manage your time, because time is one of the most valuable resources you have. If you don't decide how to use it, something else will decide for you.

Task Management: Using the Eisenhower Matrix

"What is important is seldom urgent, and what is urgent is seldom important."

Dwight Eisenhower

Eisenhower Matrix

	Urgent	Not Urgent
Important	**DO IT** Things with clear deadlines and consequences for not taking immediate action. **Examples** • Finishing a client project • Submitting a draft article • Responding to some emails • Picking up your sick kid from school	**SCHEDULE IT** Activities without a set deadline that bring you closer to your goals. Easy to procrastinate on. **Examples** • Strategic planning • Professional development • Networking • Exercise
Not Important	**DELEGATE IT** Things that need to be done, but don't require your specific skills. Busy work. **Examples** • Uploading blog posts • Scheduling • Responding to some emails • Meal prep	**DELETE IT** Distractions that make you feel worse afterward. Can be okay but only in moderation. **Examples** • Social media • Watching TV • Video games • Eating junk food

Illustration 19

Once you've established balance in how you manage your time, the next step is deciding how to work through the tasks. Task management is about focus in the moment—choosing actions intentionally instead of reacting to whatever feels loud or urgent. One of the most practical tools for this is the Eisenhower Matrix, also known as the urgent–important matrix. It helps you sort tasks by answering two simple questions:

- **Is this important?**
- **Is this urgent?**

Every task fit into one of four categories. Each category requires a different response—not more effort, but better judgment. Let's break these down.

Urgent and Important – *Do It*

These tasks require immediate attention and have clear consequences if ignored. They often involve deadlines, problems, or responsibilities that directly affect outcomes. These tasks should be addressed promptly—but not allowed to crowd out important work that prevents future urgency. Living exclusively in this quadrant leads to stress. The goal isn't to eliminate urgency, but to prevent everything from becoming urgent.

Important but Not Urgent – *Schedule It*

These tasks matter deeply but don't demand immediate action. This is where long-term progress happens—planning, preparation, health, learning, and relationship-building. This quadrant is easy to neglect because nothing is on fire. Yet this is where Balanced Achievers spend most of their time. Scheduling these tasks intentionally prevents future crises and preserves momentum.

Urgent but Not Important – *Delegate It*

These tasks feel pressing but don't require your specific attention or expertise. They often interrupt focus and pull you away from higher-impact work. Whenever possible, delegate, automate, or minimize these tasks. Doing everything yourself may feel productive, but it quietly drains energy and attention.

Neither Urgent nor Important – *Delete It*

These tasks add little value and often masquerade as productivity. They don't move you closer to your goals and don't need to be done at all. Eliminating low-value tasks isn't avoidance—it's clarity. Removing noise creates space for meaningful work.

How This Fits the PRS System

The Eisenhower Matrix doesn't replace time management—it builds on it.

- Time management helps you maintain balance and direction over days and weeks.
- Task management helps you make clear decisions in the moment.

Used together, they reduce reactivity and protect momentum. You stop chasing urgency and start choosing impact. Time maintenance sets the foundation. Task management sharpens execution. Together, they help you move forward with clarity, balance, and control.

To see how time and task management support each other, here's a simple snapshot of how I approach a typical day—not as a prescription, but as an illustration of intentional decision-making.

I start by grounding the day in Priority 1—the work that directly supports my responsibilities and stability. Within that time block, I use task management tools like the Eisenhower Matrix to decide what actually deserves attention now versus what can wait or be delegated. Urgent and important items get handled first, while important but non-urgent work gets scheduled intentionally instead of postponed indefinitely.

Once Priority 1 is protected, I move into Priority 2—efforts that don't pay off immediately but build long-term momentum. Here, task management becomes even more critical. Without structure, these tasks are easy to avoid. By identifying what's important but not urgent, I ensure progress happens without turning everything into a crisis.

Finally, I leave room for Priority 3—relationships, rest, and personal time. These moments aren't filler. They're maintenance. I don't use the Eisenhower Matrix to optimize this time; I protect it by not allowing low-value tasks to leak into it.

Some days will be heavier in one priority than another. That's normal. Time management sets the container. Task management determines what fills it. Together, they prevent burnout, reduce reactivity, and keep progress aligned with what actually matters. When time management and task management work together, you stop reacting to life and start directing it—with clarity guiding your choices, balance protecting your energy, and momentum carrying you forward.

Risk Responses

"It is well known that "problem avoidance" is an important part of problem solving. Instead of solving the problem you go upstream and alter the system so that the problem does not occur in the first place."
Edward de Bono

Not every problem is meant to be solved. Some challenges don't disappear no matter how much effort, intelligence, or planning you apply. But even when a problem can't be eliminated, you still have power. You can choose how you respond. That's what risk responses are in PRS.

They're not about fear. They're not about control. They're about clarity—knowing what deserves your energy, what doesn't, and how to keep moving forward without constantly draining yourself. Risk responses protect your balance and preserve momentum because they prevent two things that wreck progress fast:

- **Fighting reality**. Trying to force outcomes that won't change.
- **Wasting effort**. Pouring energy into problems the wrong way.

There are four primary ways to respond to risk: **avoid, mitigate, transfer, and accept.** Each has a place. The skill is choosing the one that fits the situation in front of you.

Risk Avoidance: Remove the Risk

Avoidance means eliminating the activity, environment, or pattern that creates the risk in the first place. This is the cleanest response when it's available. Avoidance isn't weakness. It's strategy. If something consistently produces harm, instability, or relapse, walking away can be the most disciplined form of problem-solving. You're not running. You're refusing to keep paying a price that isn't worth it. When the risk outweighs the benefit, avoidance protects progress instead of draining it.

Examples:

- If gambling is your trigger, you avoid casinos.
- If a relationship repeatedly turns toxic, you stop reopening the door.

- If a habit wrecks your health, you remove access and redesign your environment.

Risk Mitigation: Reduce the Impact

When you can't remove a risk, your next move is to reduce the damage it can cause.

Mitigation doesn't make the problem vanish—it keeps it from becoming a crisis. This is where you build buffers and safeguards: routines, boundaries, backup plans, emergency resources, skill-building, prevention. In PRS terms, mitigation is how you stay steady while life stays unpredictable. Mitigation preserves balance while letting you continue forward.

Examples:

- Building an emergency fund so a surprise bill doesn't become panic
- Establishing recovery and rest rituals so hard seasons don't become burnout
- Creating structure around known weak spots (time, attention, spending, sleep)

Risk Transfer: Share the Load

Transfer means shifting part of the risk to something outside of you—another person, a system, a structure, a community. In business, it can look like insurance or contracts. In real life, it often looks like something simpler and more human support from others. Transfer doesn't mean avoiding responsibility. It means recognizing the truth: some things are too heavy to carry alone. When pressure stays concentrated on one person, burnout becomes inevitable. Transfer spreads the weight. If PRS had a hidden superpower, it's this: the right support system can reduce risk faster than raw motivation ever will.

Examples:

- Asking for help instead of silently drowning
- Delegating what doesn't require you
- Building accountability so progress doesn't depend on willpower
- Leaning into community when life gets unstable

Risk Acceptance: Carrying What Cannot Be Changed

Acceptance is the hardest response—and the most misunderstood. Acceptance does not mean approval. It does not mean giving up. It means acknowledging that some risks cannot be avoided, reduced, or transferred—and deciding how you will live anyway. Some realities are permanent. Fighting them doesn't eliminate the pain—it multiplies it.

Examples:

- Living with a chronic illness that requires ongoing management, not a cure
- Accepting the limits of another person's behavior when change isn't within your control
- Carrying grief after loss without trying to fix or rush it
- Acknowledging a permanent life constraint—disability, past trauma, irreversible decisions—and building forward anyway

The most profound example of acceptance is loss. For anyone who has loved deeply—whether a pet, a friend, a partner, or a family member—loss is not a possibility. It's a certainty. Loving someone always includes the risk of grief. You can't mitigate that away without also eliminating love itself. You don't solve grief. You carry it.

At first, the weight feels unbearable. Over time, it changes shape. The sharp edges soften, but the imprint remains. Healing does not mean forgetting—it means learning how to hold both love and loss at the same time. Risk acceptance is choosing to live fully despite knowing the cost. It is not passive resignation; it is courageous acknowledgment of reality. In PRS, acceptance prevents endless struggle against what cannot be changed—and frees your energy to keep moving forward without denial or collapse.

Recalibration: When Plans Break, Adjust Without Collapsing

Here's the missing piece that makes risk responses practical: even when you choose the right response, life can still hit hard. Plans stall. Timelines break. Progress gets interrupted. PRS doesn't ask you to start over or quit. It asks you to recalibrate. Recalibration is what you do when your original plan no longer fits reality. Ask:

- What changed?
- What still matters?
- What needs to be restructured—timeline, support, expectations, or strategy?

Then you rebuild the plan in smaller steps, set new checkpoints, and keep moving without pretending nothing happened. This is how you preserve momentum without burning out. You don't lose the progress you made—you adjust the route.

Personal Example: When One Person Changes a Life

"The quality of your relationships determines the quality of your life."
E. Perel

When people hear risk responses, they often think about money, safety, or major life decisions. But some of the most important risk responses show up much earlier—during moments when survival, identity, and belonging are on the line.

What happened to me when I first came to this country wasn't a problem I could solve in a single day. It was a high-risk environment: a new country, a new language, a new culture—with no control, no familiarity, and no tools. I couldn't avoid it. I couldn't power through it. And most importantly, I couldn't fix it alone.

What I needed—and what ultimately allowed me to adapt—was a combination of mitigation, transfer, and acceptance. More than anything, I needed a support system.

This story is written as a tribute to my first teacher and mentor, Dr. Richard Singletary, who has since passed. Without his guidance, patience, and compassion, I would not have been able to adjust—let alone thrive. This section exists because of him.

It's possible to have determination, intelligence, and grit. But without support, even the strongest foundations crack. You can't build a house—or a life—by yourself. In a very real sense, it takes a village. That was true for me the moment I walked into a second-grade classroom in America.

In 1989, after only a few weeks in the U.S., I started school. I didn't speak a single word of English and was completely unfamiliar with the culture. Back home in the Philippines, breakfast meant warm pandesal from the local bakery. That morning, my mom served me cereal and milk—something I had never had before. While my clothes and lunchbox looked American—Ghostbusters and Ninja Turtles—my lunch did not. She packed Filipino food.

I was enrolled in an English as a Second Language (ESL) program at Shea Terrace Elementary and rode the bus for children with special needs. I was the only one on it. When I stepped off the bus, the other kids stared, laughed, and pointed. I didn't understand their words, but I understood their body language.

That first day, I instinctively tried to go to the ESL classroom I had visited the week before—the only place that felt familiar. When staff stopped me, I panicked and ran. They chased me around the school until they caught me, kicking and screaming, and dragged me into a regular English-speaking classroom. Eventually, they called Dr. Singletary—my ESL teacher, who spoke Tagalog—to calm me down.

I sat there while everyone stared at me like I had two heads. I couldn't understand a word being said. I felt like a zoo exhibit. Then came the stomach cramps—intense, twisting, desperate. I raised my hand, gesturing frantically and speaking in Tagalog to explain that I needed to use the bathroom. No one understood. And then it happened. I defecated in my pants and on the chair. Right there, in front of everyone. The class erupted—pointing, laughing, disgusted. Turns out the milk I'd had that morning was spoiled. My mom and I didn't know what to look for on expiration dates.

Now I wasn't just the foreign kid. I was the foreign kid who pooped himself in class.

But the day wasn't over. Later, a student turned around and flipped me the middle finger. I had no idea what it meant—so I returned the gesture, thinking it was a game. At recess, a group of boys came over—pushing, shoving, testing me. They didn't know I grew up in the slums of Cavite City. I grew up fighting. Survival wasn't optional.

A full fight broke out. We all ended up in the principal's office—bruised and bloodied. Thankfully, no one was suspended. We were just kids, and this was an extraordinary situation. All of that on day one.

So, what kept me going? My ESL classroom. That room became my safe space. My sanctuary. It was a community of kids from around the world, all trying to adapt together. We helped each other learn, translate, and survive. Within three to four months, I learned English and eventually became one of the lead student mentors for new ESL students. Ensuring no one else had to go through what I did.

And I owe so much of that to Dr. Singletary. Thank you for your guidance, your patience, and your heart. Your impact lives on through every life you touched—especially mine. You are missed and never forgotten.

Dream Solving

"The best way to escape from a problem is to solve it."
Brendan Francis

We spend a third of our lives sleeping, and more importantly, resting. Sleep is crucial for overall health as it allows the body and brain to rest, repair, and consolidate memories, with different sleep stages serving unique functions for physical restoration, cognitive processing, and optimal well-being.

Each cycle typically takes around 90 minutes with eight hours of sleep taking about three cycles. First, we enter light sleep for one to five minutes. It's easy to wake someone up at this stage. The second stage of sleep, deeper sleep, lasts 10–25 minutes. Muscles are more relaxed, and brain activity slows down. Third, we enter deepest sleep for 20–40 minutes. It's very hard to wake someone at this stage when the body is actively repairing and regrowing tissues, building bone and muscle, and strengthening the immune system. The last cycle is rapid eye movement, REM sleep, lasting 10-60 minutes is when we dream.

Dreaming Yourself Awake by Alan Wallace explores the practice of lucid dreaming, combining Western techniques with the profound insights of Tibetan Buddhist dream yoga. The book shows how to use your dreams to enhance creativity, solve problems, and gain deeper self-knowledge through intentional dream manipulation and exploration within the dream state. Using this concept, sleep becomes an efficiency tool. For example, if you have a big job interview coming up, you can mentally prepare yourself with questions or scenarios that may arise through lucid dreaming.

First, let's look at two types of dreams. Lucid dreams are where you know that you are dreaming and may even control the dream's narrative to some extent. Just think about Leonardo DiCaprio's character, Cobb, in *Inception*. While we're unlikely to achieve his degree of powers in our dreams, with hard work small feats are possible.

Vivid dreams are dreams that feel very real and detailed, often with strong sensory experiences. Have you ever had a dream of your teeth falling out, usually while you are brushing your teeth or just standing in front of a mirror? Typically, you see these scenes in scary movies. That moment feels so real, and you remember every detail of the moment. In this case, it expresses a strong emotion like fear or shock, and you eventually wake up. Lucid dreams can be vivid dreams as well, but in this aspect the dreamer realizes they are just dreaming and the possibilities become endless. It requires a lot of patience and discipline to achieve.

In essence there is a practice to do before bed that involves relaxing and meditating before falling asleep while focusing on what you want to dream about. For example, that would be the upcoming interview you are getting ready for. Start playing scenarios in your mind of how it will go, either good or bad. Next, relax every part of your body and focus on your breathing, and visually see your breath entering and exiting your body. Doing this several times before going to sleep should help start the process of lucid dreaming. Don't be discouraged if you are unsuccessful. This sounds easier than it is. Any little distraction will cause you to lose focus, like the baby crying or the dog barking, and you will have to start over.

From experience, it takes about an hour or two to go through the motions on a good try. So, if your sleep schedule is from 11PM to 7AM, aim to start around 9PM. Keep track of the lucid dream process with a dream journal. Most of us dream almost every night, but we just don't remember it. So, if you remember a dream, write it down immediately while your dream is fresh because we can forget them in a matter of minutes.

Let me share my experience with this concept. I managed to make it work twice within the first week of practice with major dedication and discipline. I did not always get what I was trying to pre-dream about, like preparing for that job interview, but I started noticing I was lucid dreaming. That is only half the battle, let me tell you. The author suggested the first thing to try in lucid dreaming is flying because one needs to differentiate between reality and dreaming. This is because gravity does not exist in dreams. My first couple of flights did not bode well. I managed to don a cape like Superman to help with the task. I was ready. I started running really fast and managed to get some flight like a chicken but broke my face on the ground many times. I did get higher and flew longer after some practice, but nothing like in the movies. I definitely need more practice when I have some time. Suggests practicing these on the weekends when you can sleep in.

Stoicism

"Know first who you are, and then adorn yourself accordingly."
Epictetus

Stoicism, to me, is not about suppressing emotion or pretending life doesn't affect you. It's about identity. Who am I? What do I stand for? And what lines do I refuse to cross—regardless of circumstance?

Most people move through life reacting out of habit, impulse, or pressure. They do what feels necessary in the moment, even when it contradicts their values. Stoicism challenges that pattern. It asks you to define your character before chaos shows up—so when pressure arrives, you already know who you are.

The mind travels everywhere you go. A monk may appear calm whether he's in a quiet temple in Tibet or navigating the chaos of New York City. That calm doesn't come from the environment—it comes from discipline built over time. His composure isn't accidental. It's practiced. But Stoicism isn't reserved for monks.

Think about everyday moments when composure slips. Have you ever reacted emotionally because someone cut you off in traffic, honked at you, or made an offensive gesture? In those moments, we're not losing discipline—we're losing composure. We allow a stranger, someone who will never matter again, to dictate our emotional state. Stoicism puts that power back where it belongs.

It teaches us to separate what is within our control from what isn't. You can't control other people's behavior. You can control your response. That distinction alone eliminates an enormous amount of unnecessary stress, anger, and wasted energy. But Stoicism goes deeper than emotional regulation. It is a moral framework.

Consider the earlier example involving financial need. A committed student of Stoicism—guided by integrity and a clear moral compass—would never genuinely entertain the idea of robbing a bank, no matter how severe the financial pressure. Not because it's risky. Not because they might get caught. But because it violates who they are.

Stoicism prioritizes virtue over convenience. Honesty over desperation. Character over short-term gain. When your identity is clearly defined, many choices disappear. You don't debate them. You don't rationalize them. They are simply not options.

This is why Stoicism aligns so closely with effective problem-solving. It reduces internal conflict. It removes emotional noise. It keeps you anchored when fear, urgency, or temptation try to pull you off course.

Our thoughts, actions, attitudes, and decisions shape our stability and effectiveness. Too often, we exhaust ourselves worrying about outcomes we can't control or chasing solutions that compromise our values. Stoicism teaches us to focus only on what we can influence— our effort, our decisions, and our integrity—and to let go of the rest.

When decisions align with core values, clarity increases. Stress decreases. Momentum becomes sustainable. You won't always feel calm. You won't always feel confident. Stoicism doesn't promise that. What it offers instead is something more durable: the ability to move forward without betraying yourself. And that, more than any technique or tactic, is what keeps balance intact over the long run.

The Three R's: Rest, Recover, Reset

"Problems do not go away. They must be worked through or else they remain, forever a barrier to the growth and development of the spirit."
M. Scott Peck

We often glorify the grind. Push through. Hustle harder. But here's the truth—even machines overheat. And unlike machines, we carry emotional, physical, and spiritual weight. There's no shame in slowing down. Sometimes the strongest move is taking a moment to pause, breathe, and reconnect with yourself.

When dealing with really hard problems, tough challenges, and major changes, sometimes it may take several attempts to find a desirable solution. This is when the three Rs become important. In my experience as you are making strides in completing goals and tasks, nothing is more debilitating than burnout. Even when you have the best tools, sharpest strategies, and an unstoppable mindset, if you're running on fumes, everything eventually falls apart. That's why I live by a simple but powerful philosophy: Rest. Recover. Reset. Without them, nothing else in this book works the way it should.

Rest

Rest isn't just sleep—though sleep is critical. Rest means taking time away from the chaos to allow your mind and body to settle. It's a conscious act of stepping back from decision-making, noise, and pressure.

When I was juggling cybersecurity deadlines, side businesses, and family life with six kids, I used to feel guilty for resting. Like I was falling behind. But over time I learned that rest is a strategic investment, not a weakness. Whether it's five minutes of silence, a walk outside, or putting your phone down for the evening—rest is how we rebuild the parts of ourselves we constantly use.

Recover

Recovery is deeper than rest. It's where healing happens. Think of recovery as the body and mind syncing back to neutral after stress or exhaustion. This might be physical (working out then stretching), emotional (venting or journaling), or spiritual (prayer or quiet time). It's about giving yourself permission to restore energy and perspective.

After a grueling military deployment, my body came home—but my mind didn't. I had to relearn how to feel peace, how to breathe without tension, and how to trust my gut again. Recovery was not optional—it was survival. We have to be intentional about it.

Reset

Finally, you're ready to reset. This is where you return to your purpose, refreshed and realigned. Resetting doesn't always mean changing your goals—it means recalibrating your approach with clarity and calm. You're not reacting anymore. You're back in control.

For me, a reset often looks like stepping back after a heavy stretch, reviewing what worked and what didn't, and deliberately choosing how I want to move forward. Sometimes that means re-planning the week. Other times it's as simple as acknowledging, that project was hard—but I'm still here, and I can continue.

Resetting might look like re-planning your week, recommitting to your goals after a tough season, or simply saying, okay, let's try again. It's how you begin again—stronger, wiser, and more focused.

Maintenance is where systems become sustainable and growth becomes integrated. PRS was never meant to be something you do once—it's something you practice, revisit, and refine. The goal isn't to stay balanced at all times, but to recognize imbalance sooner and return to alignment faster. That's how clarity compounds, momentum stabilizes, and confidence becomes earned rather than assumed.

Sustain Your System

"Discipline is the bridge between motion and mastery."

This practice is designed to take 10–15 minutes total. Don't overthink your answers. Maintenance makes the difference between progress that lasts and progress that fades. Your system—like any well-tuned vehicle—requires regular check-ins, small adjustments, and occasional refueling. When you maintain your system, you preserve momentum, protect balance, and keep your journey steady through every season. Your progress isn't a single race; it's a lifetime drive—smooth, deliberate, and unstoppable when cared for with intention.

The techniques below will help you sustain your momentum and keep the PRS running smoothly long after the motivation fades.

Step 1 – Once a week, review your goals, schedule, and stress levels. You can use a journal, digital notebook, or the PRS Workbook section to log this review. Think of it as your oil change—small, consistent maintenance that prevents big breakdowns later. Ask yourself:

- What worked this week?
- What broke down?
- What can I adjust for next week?

Step 2 – Take 10 minutes at the end of each day to check your internal dashboard. Keeps these in mind. Over time, you'll start to see patterns—where your energy spikes, when burnout looms, and how your balance shifts.

- Did I act in alignment with my mission and motive today? Yes/No
- Did I need to switch quadrants? Yes/No
- Did I advance or drift? Yes/No

Step 3 – Make time for a rest stop reset Just like a long drive, no vehicle can go full speed forever. Pausing prevents burnout and extends your journey. Schedule recovery days or blocks of time where you do nothing related to goals or productivity.

These "rest stops" help you:

- Refill your emotional and mental fuel.
- Reconnect with family, nature, or spirituality.
- Reflect on gratitude rather than goals.

Step 4 –. Acknowledging forward motion builds momentum. Every mile counts. Pick one area of your life—career, health, relationships—and track progress weekly or monthly. Celebrate small wins as milestones. Write them down, no matter how small. Here are a couple examples:

"I handled stress better this week."
"I stuck to my morning routine three days in a row."

Step 5 – Calibration keeps your PRS vehicle tuned to your current reality. Remember, growth requires adjustments. Once a month, revisit your mission, motive, and method. Ask yourself:

- Does my mission still feel aligned with who I'm becoming?
- Has my motive evolved with new experiences?
- Is my method still efficient—or do I need to update it?

KEY INSIGHTS FOR CHAPTER 8

- **Effectively using the PRS requires both structured strategies and mental discipline.** By consistently applying these tools and techniques, you transform everyday problems into meaningful opportunities for personal and professional growth. These mechanisms transform us into efficient problem solvers—empowering us to execute with purpose and keep building momentum.

- **Starting with why should come first.** Focusing on the why becomes the guiding force that shapes decisions, actions, and direction in our lives. When you know why something matters, it is much easier to endure roadblocks and setbacks. If you're lost, unmotivated, or stuck in inaction, chances are you've lost connection with your Why.

- **Mastering skills is a continuous journey.** Willpower and determination often surpass initial skill levels in developing true expertise. Achieving mastery typically requires extensive and consistent practice (around 10,000 hours). Teaching a skill confirms mastery; if you cannot teach clearly, you may need to spend more time learning or practicing.

- **SWOT analysis for personal growth** A personal SWOT analysis offers a clear framework to assess your current self before setting or adjusting goals. Identifying your strengths and weaknesses builds self-awareness and helps you play to your advantages. Recognizing opportunities and threats allows you to anticipate challenges and make strategic life decisions. Reassessing your SWOT regularly ensures your personal growth stays aligned with your evolving goals and circumstances.

- **SMART goals provide clear direction.** Goals must be specific, clearly defining exactly what you aim to achieve. Make goals measurable to track progress effectively. Ensure goals are achievable, considering available resources and time. Keep goals relevant to align with broader personal or professional objectives. Set time-bound deadlines to maintain urgency and accountability.

- **Effective time management maximizes productivity.** Prioritize tasks by direct benefits, indirect benefits, and leisure or routine tasks. Value your time realistically, delegate or combine tasks to optimize productivity. Thoughtful prioritization ensures every hour is spent meaningfully.

- **The Eisenhower matrix streamlines task management.** Clearly categorize tasks based on urgency and importance. Focus immediate efforts on tasks with the highest urgency and importance. Delegating and minimizing lower-priority tasks frees resources for critical activities.

- **Strategic risk management transforms uncertainty into manageable opportunities.** Choose between risk avoidance, mitigation, transfer, or acceptance according to the situation. Document and manage risks systematically through structured action plans.

- **Dream solving enhances creative problem re-solving.** Lucid dreaming can mentally rehearse scenarios and solve problems creatively. Disciplined practice and patience unlock the powerful subconscious problem re-solving potential of dreaming. Leveraging dream states aids emotional preparation, clarity, and decision-making.

- **Stoicism cultivates resilience and clarity.** Differentiate clearly between what you can control (thoughts, actions) and what you cannot (external events). Maintain emotional discipline and stability to effectively handle life's challenges. Stoicism fosters purposeful action and inner calm, reducing stress and anxiety.

- **Rest, recovery, and reset build sustainable progress.** Rest incorporates intentional pauses to prevent burnout and regain clarity. Use recovery as a tool to rebuild energy, focus, and emotional strength. Resetting aligns you with your goals and fosters long-term resilience.

My Story of Transformation

"What we do for ourselves dies with us.
What we do for others' lives on."
Albert Pine

Before we close out, I need to share my story—not because I want sympathy, but because I want context. I want my children, my grandchildren (who may never meet me), and anyone reading this to understand where my mindset came from. PRS didn't come out of a seminar or a podcast. It came out of survival.

When you grow up day-to-day wondering where your next meal is coming from, efficiency isn't a productivity hack—it's life. You learn to move fast, waste nothing, and solve problems before they become emergencies. That's the soil PRS grew in.

My Story: How PRS Was Forged

"Necessity is the mother of invention."

Plato

From Scarcity to Strategy

I was born in 1981 in Cavite City, Philippines—a densely packed coastal town where struggle wasn't occasional; it was normal. My mom was only sixteen when she had me. Soon after, she left me with my father's family to escape abuse, and my uncle practically raised me. We lived ten people deep in a shack on stilts, built to survive monsoon floods. One bedroom. One shared kitchen. No running water. No plumbing. No refrigerator. No air conditioning. Electricity, mostly for lights and a fan.

Every day we carried buckets from a public water station. We cooked on a small gas stove. We showered outside. When the rain came hard, the streets flooded so high we swam through them—dirty water, sewage, who knows what else—because that was just the neighborhood. Mosquitoes and cockroaches weren't gross; they were roommates. We slept on woven mats, under a thin net, because bugs didn't ask permission. I once got bitten on the eyelid and couldn't see right for days.

We didn't have birthday parties. I didn't own toys. So, I made them—tin cans turned into cars, string for a steering wheel, coins wrapped in candy wrappers for a game of *sipa*, marbles, in the dirt.

We were super broke, but we were creative. We had nothing, but we had the will to survive.

My father drove a tricycle taxi. My grandfather drove a jeepney. In a house of ten, only two people brought in income. Most days, there was barely enough after gas and maintenance. Waste wasn't an option. Every coin mattered. Every scrap mattered. And everybody contributed—including the kids. We scavenged bottles and scrap from garbage piles just to earn a few pesos.

Those years didn't just shape my circumstances—they shaped my instincts. Humility. Hunger. Awareness. The ability to adapt. The habit of moving fast when an opportunity appears because you don't know when the next one will come.

My mother's story was even harder—abandoned young, orphaned young, working as a child, dropping out of school early just to survive. When I was six, she came back into my life full-time. It was comforting and confusing at the same time. Then, when I turned eight, she married an American serviceman, and we moved to the United States.

Leaving the Philippines was the saddest and scariest day of my life. I cried when we left our family home. And when we arrived in Portsmouth, Virginia, the culture shock hit like a wall. New language. New rules. New people. I couldn't understand anyone, and I didn't know how the systems worked. I struggled in school academically, socially, emotionally—bullying, self-doubt, anxiety, and the invisible weight of a childhood built on scarcity.

But even then, I was learning something that would become PRS years later: not all problems are the same. Some require immediate action. Some require patience. And some are changes you don't solve—you adapt to. I didn't have those words back then, but I felt the difference in my bones.

Orders and Obstacles

By the time I turned 18, life in the States still wasn't what I imagined. I'd already been through a youth rehab program at 15—army-style drills, trade work, and learning how to stay out of trouble. I tried community college, but I couldn't afford it. I was young, angry, and broke. After a fistfight with my stepfather, I got kicked out of the house and had two options: sink or survive. I bounced from job to job—Holiday Inn, Chick-fil-A, Dunkin', Food Lion, Aramark—getting fired or laid off like it was routine.

Eventually, I joined the U.S. Air Force in August 1999. Not because I dreamed of wearing the uniform, but because it was the only door still open. From day one, it was about proving something—not just to others, but to myself. The military gave me discipline and structure— but it also gave me pressure, instability, and a version of myself that stayed in motion to avoid what I felt. Looking back, I didn't have PRS language yet, but I was living the pattern: moving fast, staying busy, calling it progress, while skipping the parts that would've healed me. I didn't know it then, but I was stuck in one of my future quadrants— impulsive action without purpose—always moving, never pausing, never processing. And that's exactly why I needed a system. Because intensity isn't the same thing as direction.

Lost in the Civilian Loop

My contract ended and I left service in November 2007 and stayed in the Air Force Reserve until 2017. The timing couldn't have been worse. The 2008 recession hit, the job I expected fell through, and I ended up delivering pizzas at Papa John's—eating pizza every day just to survive. Even with roommates, my savings dried up fast.

I had to rebuild—again. And this is where support systems mattered. A buddy from the Pentagon called me and helped me land on my feet. I found my way into defense contracting and IT, and my security clearance opened doors that would've been locked otherwise. I took whatever work I could get, trying to provide, stay afloat, and figure out who I was without the uniform.

Life didn't slow down. Marriage. Divorce. Remarriage. School. Work. Reserves. Raising kids. Blending families. I became a father six times over. I earned my associates, bachelors, and master's degrees. And I carried stress levels that would break most people—until my body started telling the truth. I developed physical and mental problems. Some days I couldn't get out of bed. Some nights I couldn't sleep. I was breaking down quietly, invisibly. I didn't even understand it as a breakdown. I just thought I was tired. That's when reflection finally caught up with motion.

I started seeing patterns: work hard, burn out, crash, reset, recover. Rinse then repeats. I didn't want to live like that anymore. I wanted answers—not just to fix symptoms, but to understand the machine underneath the chaos. My focus shifted to observing and tracking what triggered me, calmed me, caused me to spiral, and helped me return to center.

I didn't call it PRS yet. I didn't have quadrant names, acronyms, or diagrams. But the foundation was forming.

What I realized was simple: pain without reflection becomes a cycle. So, I built a system—not to make life perfect, but to make it navigable. Something that could still work even when I didn't feel strong, focused, or in control. That system became what you're holding now.

And to my children, my grandchildren, and anyone reading this who feels like they'll never make it out—listen to me: you can. I'm proof. You're not stuck. This isn't the end. It's the beginning. You just haven't learned how to re-solve the problem yet. I didn't start with privilege. I started with survival. And I turned that into perspective.

Writing This Book

"Knowing is not enough; we must apply."
Johann Wolfgang von Goethe

I didn't just create PRS and then explain it. I had to use it. Writing this book became the proving ground—the place where every component of PRS was tested under real pressure, real fatigue, real doubt, and real-life constraints. What follows the application of PRS to my journey in creating this book. I hope you find it helpful seeing the process in action.

Mission – The Destination

Every journey starts with knowing where you're going. When I first sat down to write this book, I was overwhelmed. Not for lack of ideas, but for too many of them. Notebooks filled with lessons, stories, frameworks, and half-formed concepts surrounded me—but there was no clear direction. I knew I wanted to help people who felt stuck, frustrated, or lost. People like me. But I didn't yet know how. Everything changed the moment I clarified my mission. This wasn't about publishing a book. It was about building a system that could guide someone from chaos to clarity. Once that destination became clear, decisions stopped competing with each other. The fog lifted. Forward motion finally had a direction. The best part is that it fit me leaving a legacy which is my ultimate Why.

Motive – The Driver

A destination without motive won't move you very far. My motive wasn't abstract. It came from lived experience—years of rebuilding, repeated burnout, six kids to raise, and the quiet pressure of wanting to prove that growth is possible even when life doesn't start fair. I wasn't trying to impress anyone. I was trying to leave something useful behind. Once mission and motive locked together, hesitation lost its grip. Energy replaced doubt. On the hardest days, when motivation was low, motive carried me forward anyway.

Method – The Vehicle

Direction without structure leads nowhere. Once the mission was clear, I built the vehicle. Outlines. Chapter scaffolds. Framework maps. Flowcharts. I gave all those scattered ideas lanes to travel in. This is where I had to use AI as a partner—not a replacement for thinking, but a co-driver. A way to test ideas, stress logic, and sharpen clarity. The structure contained the chaos. Creativity stopped leaking through the cracks. Progress became repeatable instead of sporadic.

Mindset – The Fuel

Even the best vehicle won't move without fuel. Some days I felt energized. Other days, it felt like pushing a car uphill. I learned quickly that waiting for motivation was a losing strategy. Discipline mattered more. Showing up every day—even for fifteen minutes—was the difference between dreaming and doing. Mindset became my daily tune-up. I stopped chasing big wins and focused on winning the day. Consistency replaced intensity. Small forward motion became enough.

Model – The Dashboard

Halfway through the process, I realized something uncomfortable. I was living inside my quadrant model. Some days I was the Reflective Thinker, over-analyzing. Other days, the Impulsive Actor, rushing edits. Occasionally, the Fearful Avoider, hesitating to move forward at all. Awareness changed everything. Once I could see my behavioral posture, I could correct it. The model became my dashboard—showing me when I was drifting, over-correcting, or moving in balance. Awareness turned reaction into control.

Movement – The Engine

Momentum didn't arrive in one dramatic surge. It built slowly through the 4A Framework—anticipate, activate, advance, achieve. When holidays, work, or life disruptions knocked me off rhythm, I returned to those four stages to regain traction. Anticipate challenges. Activate small actions. Advance with consistency. Achieve steady output. Momentum became the heartbeat of the project—not loud, not flashy, but reliable.

Mapping – The Navigation

No journey stays on course without adjustments. As feedback came in from editors, peers, and reviewers, my ego got tested. Hard choices followed—what to cut, what to rewrite, what to defend. Mapping tools helped me stay objective. I used simple decision filters: Does this serve the mission? Yes or no. Why does this feel off? What problem am I actually solving? Critique stopped feeling like rejection. It became a tool for redirection.

Maintenance – The Toolkit

Maintenance isn't exciting—but it's essential. By the final drafts, maintenance carried the project. Version tracking. Daily journaling. Edit logs. Backups. Simple habits that kept the system running when creativity dipped. Like changing oil or checking tire pressure, it wasn't glamorous—but it prevented burnout and breakdown.

Mastery – Becoming the System

When I finally typed the last line, I realized something important. The real transformation wasn't the book. It was me. PRS didn't just describe change—I lived it. Each component quietly reshaped how I thought, worked, and recovered. Mission gave direction. Motive supplied energy. Method provided structure. Mindset sustained effort. The model brought awareness. Momentum kept progress alive. Mapping allowed adaptation. Maintenance ensured longevity. PRS isn't just a system for others. It's a mirror of growth. When all eight components work together, motion becomes intentional and transformation becomes inevitable. You don't just move forward—you evolve. With clarity as your compass and balance as your road, you become both the driver and the destination.

CHAPTER 10

Conclusion & Moving Forward

"The only real mistake is the one from which we learn nothing."
Henry Ford

Congratulations. If you've made it this far, you've done more than finish a book. You've slowed down long enough to examine how you think, how you move, and how you respond when life pushes back. That alone puts you ahead of where you started. Most people never pause long enough to understand themselves, let alone change their patterns. You did.

This book was never about eliminating problems. Life doesn't work that way. Problems, challenges, and change are constants. What can change is how you meet them. PRS exists to give you clarity when things feel chaotic, balance when momentum feels shaky, and a way forward when you're unsure of your next step. Not through motivation or hype, but through structure, awareness, and intentional movement.

Along the way, you learned that not all adversity is the same. Problems require logic. Challenges demand persistence. Change calls for adaptability. Treating them all the same leads to frustration and burnout. Treating them correctly creates traction. PRS helps you make that distinction—and respond accordingly.

You learned to recognize your default behaviors through the quadrant model. Not to label yourself, but to gain awareness. Fearful avoidance, overthinking, impulsive action—none of these are failures. They're signals. Feedback. Once you can see them, you can adjust. Awareness doesn't fix everything, but it gives you the power to choose your next move instead of reacting automatically.

You were introduced to movement through the 4A Framework—anticipate, activate, advance, achieve. Not as a straight line, but as a cycle you'll return to again and again. Some seasons require preparation. Others demand courage. Some call for discipline. Others for reflection and maintenance. Progress doesn't come from rushing through the stages; it comes from honoring the one you're in.

You learned that momentum is built through consistency, not intensity. That mapping helps you reroute instead of quit. That maintenance keeps progress alive long after motivation fades. And that mastery isn't perfection—it's integration. The ability to use the right tool at the right time, and to return to balance faster when life knocks you off center.

Most importantly, you learned that PRS is not something you do once. It's something you practice. Some days you'll need clarity. Some days structure. Some days patience. Some days courage. The system is flexible because life is. You don't need to use every component all the time. You just need to know which one matters now. As you move forward, remember this:

- When you feel stuck, return to awareness.
- When momentum fades, return to structure.

- When fear shows up, return to intention.
- When progress feels slow, remember—you're still moving.

The goal was never to live in the Balanced Achiever quadrant permanently. That's unrealistic. The real goal is to recognize where you are, move intentionally, and return to balance faster each time. That's how growth becomes sustainable. That's how clarity compounds. That's how confidence is built—not through certainty, but through repetition.

This book was not written to tell you what to think. It was written to give you a way to think clearly when it matters most. To help you pause instead of panic. To act without burning out. To adapt without losing yourself. You don't need a perfect plan. You don't need to have it all figured out. You just need the next right move. PRS doesn't promise an easy road. It gives you a reliable vehicle. Where you drive it from here is up to you. And now—you're ready to move forward with intention.

THE PRS DAILY BLUEPRINT: TURNING INSIGHT INTO ACTION

This appendix is your tactical playbook. Its purpose is simple: to help you apply the PRS System consistently in daily life. You do not need to use every element every day. PRS was never meant to be rigid. Some seasons require action, others reflection. What matters is intentional movement — using the right tools at the right time. Use this blueprint to build clarity, balance, and momentum as you re-solve life's problems, challenges, and changes.

Morning Rituals – Set Your Foundation

How you start the day determines how you move through it.

- Wake up at a consistent time to build rhythm and discipline
- Reflect on dreams or lingering thoughts (journal or voice note)
- Make your bed — a small early win that builds momentum
- Prayer, meditation, or deep breathing to ground yourself
- Read a short affirmation, proverb, or guiding principle
- Move your body: stretch, walk, or exercise

- Eat a nourishing breakfast
- Review your goals, priorities, or quadrant focus for the day

PRS Focus: Anticipate → Mindset → Preparation

Day Planning & Focus – Move with Intention

Structure prevents overwhelm.

- Use a planner, app, or PRS journal to organize your day
- Apply the Eisenhower Matrix (urgent vs. important)
- Choose 1–2 high-impact tasks that truly matter
- Ask: *"Which quadrant am I operating from right now?"*
- Limit distractions by batching email and social media
- Schedule intentional breaks using the Rest → Recover → Reset approach

PRS Focus: Activate → Momentum → Discipline

Midday Check-In – Realign & Adjust

Midday awareness prevents burnout.

- Pause and take several deep breaths
- Stretch or take a short walk
- Ask:

- *Am I still aligned with today's mission?*
- *Has my quadrant shifted?*

- Adjust priorities if the day has changed

PRS Focus: Mapping → Adaptation

Evening Wind Down – Reflect & Recharge

Reflection turns experience into growth.

- Review the day: What worked? What didn't?
- Journal one lesson learned
- Write three things you're grateful for
- End the day with prayer, meditation, or silence
- Prepare for tomorrow (clothes, notes, mental reset)

PRS Focus: Achieve → Reflection → Recovery

Weekly Reset – Maintain Your Trajectory

Momentum is sustained weekly, not daily.

- Review your week honestly
- Identify progress and friction points
- Reassess quadrant patterns

- Celebrate consistency, not perfection
- Adjust goals or focus areas for the coming week

PRS Focus: Maintenance → Renewal

PROBLEM RE-SOLVING: DAILY WORKSHEET

Use this worksheet to start intentionally and close reflectively.

Dream Reflection

What do you remember from your dreams or waking thoughts?

Morning Gratitude

List 1–3 things you're grateful for today.

Top Priorities

What are the three most important priorities today?

Quadrant Check-In

Which quadrant are you currently in?

(Fearful Avoider · Reflective Thinker · Impulsive Actor · Balanced Achiever)

Action Steps

What 1–2 actions will help you move toward the Balanced Achiever quadrant?

Time & Task Planning

What are today's key tasks, and when will you do them?

Mindset & Focus Statement

Write one sentence that sets your intention for the day.

Evening Reflection

What went well today? What will you improve tomorrow?

INFLUENTIAL BOOKS FOR FURTHER STUDY

"A reader lives a thousand lives before he dies. The man who never reads lives only one."
George R.R. Martin

Financial

Rich Dad Poor Dad — Robert Kiyosaki

The Richest Man in Babylon — George Clason

Think and Grow Rich — Napoleon Hill

Money: Master the Game — Tony Robbins

Principles — Ray Dalio

The Total Money Makeover — Dave Ramsey

Financial Feminist — Tori Dunlap

Professional

The 10X Rule — Grant Cardone

How to Win Friends & Influence People — Dale Carnegie

The Power of Broke — Daymond John

Who Moved My Cheese? — Spencer Johnson

Yes or No — Spencer Johnson

The Five Dysfunctions of a Team — Patrick Lencioni

The 4-Hour Workweek — Tim Ferriss

Personal

The Five Love Languages — Gary Chapman

Dreaming Yourself Awake — Alan Wallace

The 7 Habits of Highly Effective People — Stephen Covey

Start With Why — Simon Sinek

Never Split the Difference — Chris Voss

168 Hours — Laura Vanderkam

Atomic Habits — James Clear

*The Subtle Art of Not Giving a F*ck* — Mark Manson

The Obstacle Is the Way — Ryan Holiday

Meditations — Marcus Aurelius

References

"We do not learn from experience... we learn from reflecting on experience."
John Dewey

Brittanica. (2025, October 11). Newton's laws of motion. Retrieved from https://www.britannica.com/science/Newtons-laws-of-motion

National Institute of Standards and Technology. Risk Management framework. Retrieved from

https://csrc.nist.gov/pubs/sp/800/37/r2/final.

Medium Nathan McCurry. (2023, November 30). The Three Ds of Success: Discipline, Determination, and Dedication. Retrieved from https://medium.com/@apriltheworkingcocker/the-three-ds-of-success-discipline-determination-and-dedication-9762e0f5189f

Malcolm Gladwell. (2011, June 7). Outliers: The Story of Success. University of California. SMART Goals. Retrieved from https://www.ucop.edu/local-human-resources/_files/performance-appraisal/How+to+write+SMART+Goals+v2.pdf

Columbia University School of Professional Studies. The Eisenhower Matrix. Retrieved from https://sps.columbia.edu/sites/default/files/2023-08/Eisenhower%20Matrix.pdf

National Institute of Standards and Technology. Risk Responses. Retrieved from https://nvlpubs.nist.gov/nistpubs/Legacy/SP/nistspecialpublication800-137.pdf

Sleep Foundation. (2025, July 25). Stages of Sleep: What Happens in a Normal Sleep Cycle. Retrieved from. https://www.sleepfoundation.org/stages-of-sleep

Forum Health Jan Rogers. Reset, Rest, and Recover: Prioritize Self Care Before Setting New Resolutions. Retrieved from https://forumhealth.com/wellness/reset-rest-and-recover-prioritize-self-care-before-setting-new-resolutions/

Tulip. What are the Five Whys? Retrieved from https://tulip.co/glossary/five-whys/

FasterCapital. (2025, March 31). Decision-making models: Choosing the Right Path — Exploring Decision-making Models. Retrieved from https://fastercapital.com/content/Decision-making-models--Choosing-the-Right-Path--Exploring-Decision-making-Models.html

Board of Innovation. (2026, January 5). 16 cognitive biases that can kill your decision making. Retrieved from https://www.boardofinnovation.com/blog/16-cognitive-biases-that-kill-innovative-thinking/

ABOUT THE AUTHOR

Michael Alcantara was born in Cavite City, Philippines, and immigrated to the United States when he was eight years old. He grew up in Portsmouth, Virginia, and graduated from Woodrow Wilson High School in 1998. After graduating, he joined the United States Air Force at age 18. He served for 18 years in Active Duty and the Reserves holding various roles and responsibilities. He has 20 years of IT skills and experience with a focus on cybersecurity governance, risk, and compliance. He holds a Bachelors in IT and a Master's in Business Administration. He is also the President and founder of the GBA Bright Futures Foundation.

He currently lives in Stafford, Virginia, with his wife, Riza, and their six kids, three dogs, and two cats. He enjoys spending time with family and friends., outdoors, learning, teaching, and educating. He believes in paying it forward, helping those around him to be the best versions of themselves and realize their full true potential.

Website: https://www.michaelalcantara.net/

www.ingramcontent.com/pod-product-compliance
Lightning Source LLC
Chambersburg PA
CBHW032018150726
47990CB00005B/2028